MEMORIAL

OF

E. K. COLLINS & HIS ASSOCIATES

TO THE

SENATE AND HOUSE OF REPRESENTATIVES

OF THE

UNITED STATES OF AMERICA.

The undersigned, contractors for carrying the United States Mail between New York and Liverpool, beg leave to call the attention of Congress to the annexed letters of the Postmaster General and the Secretary of the Navy, in regard to the increase of the Atlantic Mail service, and the proposed additional compensation for the same.

In making this communication your memorialists beg leave to present a brief statement of what they have accomplished, the circumstances which compel them to solicit additional assistance, and the public reasons which sustain their application.

We have built four steamers of an aggregate tonnage of more than 11,000 tons. These steamers have made twenty-eight voyages, with an average speed greater than has ever before been attained—surpassing that of the Cunard steamers, which have been built subsequently to ours, expressly to maintain the maritime supremacy of England.

Our steamers have been built at an expense which was unavoidable, in view of the great enterprise to which we were committed. To excel the English lines it was indispensable that we should construct larger vessels, with improved machinery. From the start, therefore, we were involved in experiments; for we could borrow neither the models, nor the machinery, nor the workmen, which were necessary to accomplish our object. England had done her best, and we were hro wn upon our own resources for doing better.

Our original proposition contemplated five steamers of 2,000 tons, and of one thousand horse-power each. Ascertaining that we could not compete successfully with the improved English Mail service by vessels of this description, we have built steamers of larger tonnage and increased power, without regard to the calls of our contract or the additional expenses involved. Relying on the national objects in view, and the national character of the enterprise, we have not been content to regard it as a commercial speculation, but have considered ourselves embarked in a contest of maritime skill and superiority. In the latter view we have been eminently successful. The Postmaster General, in his last annual report, takes official notice of the "unrivalled qualities and the speed" of the vessels of our line, and of the very satisfactory manner in which we have performed the service; establishing, in his judgment, the "superiority of American skill and enterprise in the construction of ocean steamers," and entitling us to the most favorable consideration of Congress.

But these results could be accomplished only by the most liberal outlay, without reference to the stipulated compensation for the proposed service. Hence it has ensued that our enterprise, on its present basis, must involve all who have engaged in it in heavy losses, unless we are met by Congress in a national spirit, responsive to that by which we have ourselves been actuated. Nearly one-half of our present annual compensation for the Mail service is expended in effecting insurance on our ships, the cost of which has been much enhanced by their immense tonnage, and the expensive improvements without which we could not have competed, with any hope of success, with the greatest naval power in the world.

The advantages which have resulted to our country from the prosecution of our enterprise in the manner to which we have referred, and which could not otherwise have been secured, may be briefly enumerated. We are now dividing with England the carriage of the Atlantic mails and passengers; a business of which she had a monopoly previously to the establishment of our line. The Government of the United States has now at its control, and subject to its disposal for any public purposes, whether of war or peace, the four largest and swiftest steamers in the world, supported meanwhile at little present expense to the treasury, and with a safe prospect, not only of reimbursing every dollar of immediate outlay, but of contributing not inconsiderably to the public revenue. It is proper that we should state in this connexion the facts which make it reasonable to believe that the Government will not only be reimbursed for all its expenditures in its ocean mail service, but will ultimately derive a revenue from it. The amount accruing to the Post Office Department from the postage of the ocean steamers, for the year which ended 30th June, 1851, and during the quarter which ended the 30th September, 1851, was $1,131,776 87. This sum would have been paid to the British steamers, and would have aided in keeping afloat a provisional British navy, had it not been for the policy of competition wisely adopted by the Government of the United States. It is just to assume that this sum will be increased every year, and with the increased number of trips of the American steamers the American proportion of the postages will be augmented without reference to the probable augmentation of international communication. This is, of course, daily extending, leading to a daily extension of our foreign correspondence, and consequently to our receipts from ocean postages. The increased aid, then, that we solicit, and which is indispensable to the continued prosecution of our enterprise, will impose a very inconsiderable present burden on the Treasury, and, taking the whole term of our contract, no charge whatever.

Your memorialists appeal with pride to the strength, size, and speed of their ships, not merely in view of the advantages which the country derives from them in their pacific mission of transmitting intelligence and passengers from one continent to the other, but also for their capacity of usefulness in time of war, in the transport of troops and supplies, of agents and despatches, as well as for all other naval purposes. And when, in addition to all this, we consider their inexpensive intermediate support, while they are thus in readiness and preparation for such public emergencies, we cannot permit ourselves to doubt that Congress will regard our enterprise with reference to its great public advantages and national ends, and grant us such additional facilities as may be found indispensable to its further prosecution, and the maintenance of our present admitted superiority.

We make this appeal with the greater confidence from the fact that the rival English line is sustained to every extent by the English government, and that, in a national competition, we cannot doubt the willingness of the American people to grant all reasonable and just assistance to their countrymen. We ask nothing beyond it, and we know not that we can better manifest our own disposition in this matter, and better prove that we are actuated by national and not personal motives in our appeal, than by stipulating at this time, that whatever increased facilities may be extended to us by Congress, we will readily transfer our ships at cost, with our contract, to any persons who may be acceptable to Government, and capable, in their view, of carrying out successfully an enterprise of such vital interest and importance to the American nation.

E. K. COLLINS,
For himself and associates.

Copy.

POST OFFICE DEPARTMENT,
November 15, 1851.

SIR: By their contract, the proprietors of the Collins line of steamers between New York and Liverpool, as you are aware, are required to perform only twenty voyages per annum—that is, monthly trips during four months, and semi-monthly trips eight months, of each year. In alternating, as at present, with the steamers of the Cunard line, we are informed by Mr. Collins that, by the 1st of January next, his steamers will have made seventeen trips, leaving only three voyages to be performed from the 1st January to the 27th April, the end of the contract year.

The Cunard line has now been ordered up to weekly service the year round; and deeming it highly important, therefore, that the trips on the Collins line should be increased from twenty to twenty-six a year, I have already given Mr. Collins the assurance, that if he shall see fit to run the necessary additional trips, to alternate, as at present, with the British lines through the year, and will look to Congress for compensation, I will recommend to Congress the allowance of pro rata, or such additional, pay therefor as shall be considered fair and proper under the circumstances.

It cannot be doubted that it is for the interest of the United States to afford such aid to the Collins line as will enable it to compete successfully with the British lines running in connexion therewith; and I beg leave to call your attention to the subject, in the hope that you will unite with me in such recommendation to Congress as will secure the increase of the service of the Collins line from twenty to twenty-six trips a year as a permanent arrangement.

I have the honor to be, very respectfully, your obedient servant,

(Signed) N. K. HALL,
Postmaster General.

Hon. WM. A. GRAHAM,
Secretary of the Navy.

Copy.

NAVY DEPARTMENT,
November 28, 1851.

SIR: Your letter of the 25th instant, in relation to further mail service for your steamers between New York and Liverpool, has been received.

You are informed, in reply, that this Department concurs with the Postmaster General in his requirements of additional service by the mail steamers from New York to Liverpool, as expressed by him in his letter to this Department, of which you have been furnished with a copy.

You will, therefore, be pleased to furnish a schedule of the days of sailing of the Liverpool mail steamers of your line at as early a day as practicable.

The subject relating to compensation will be referred by the Postmaster General for the consideration of Congress.

I am, very respectfully, your obedient servant,

(Signed) WM. A. GRAHAM.

EDWARD K. COLLINS, esq., *and associates, New York.*

THE

SUPREMACY OF THE SEAS,

OR FACTS, VIEWS, STATEMENTS, AND OPINIONS

RELATING TO

The American and British Steamers

BETWEEN THE U. STATES AND LIVERPOOL.

FROM AMERICAN AND BRITISH SOURCES.

WITH THE MEMORIAL OF THE PROPRIETORS OF THE NEW YORK AND LIVERPOOL LINE OF AMERICAN STEAMERS.

WASHINGTON:
PRINTED BY GIDEON AND CO.
1851.

THE SUPREMACY OF THE SEAS,

OR FACTS, VIEWS, STATEMENTS, AND OPINIONS

RELATING TO THE

AMERICAN & BRITISH STEAMERS

BETWEEN THE UNITED STATES AND LIVERPOOL.

FROM AMERICAN AND BRITISH SOURCES.

WITH THE MEMORIAL OF THE PROPRIETORS OF THE NEW YORK AND LIVERPOOL LINE OF AMERICAN STEAMERS.

WASHINGTON:
PRINTED BY GIDEON AND CO.
1851.

☞ A memorial having been presented to Congress, relating to the American line of Steamers from New York to Liverpool, it is deemed proper to present, in connexion with the same, the American and British views on the great question of supremacy of the seas, which, on both sides of the Atlantic, is now supposed to be involved in the competition of the New York and British lines. The articles here presented will be found to embody a great mass of interesting and instructive facts, and may enable the reader to form just opinions and views respecting the claims of said memorial, as well as upon the pending national contract.

MEMORIAL

OF

E. K. COLLINS AND HIS ASSOCIATES,

To the Senate and House of Representatives of the United States of America.

The undersigned, contractors for carrying the United States Mail between New York and Liverpool, respectfully ask the attention of Congress to the statements and the petition of this their memorial.

It is now about four years since your memorialists entered into a contract with the Secretary of the Navy for building five steamships, to be employed as a mail line between this country and England. At that time England enjoyed undisputed supremacy in the steam navigation of the Altantic, and monopolized the carriage of the passengers and letters of the world. In the interval that has since elapsed, your memorialists have built four steamers of the largest size, with accommodations for the comfort of passengers far exceeding every thing of the kind before known; of a speed that compares favorably with that of the steamers of the competing English lines, and which they attained only after ten years' experience; notwithstanding the inexperience and consequent inferiority of their engineers and firemen, the steamers of the American line have made the shortest passages to the westward, and, with but two exceptions, (and those of three hours only) the shortest passage to the eastward, that have ever yet been accomplished. It is admitted on both sides of the water, that the ships and their steam-machinery, are equal to the best of British build and manufacture. This success has been attained at very great expense, and under very disadvantageous circumstances.

The manufacture of machinery, much larger than had ever before been built in this country, was disproportionately expensive, (much larger than was anticipated) and the materials employed in it were better and higher-priced than were ever before used for the same purposes. The cost was still enhanced (in comparison with that of the British lines) by the high prices of labor; and the result is, that when the line is completed, so great will have been the original outlay that the insurance alone will amount to $228,000, being considerably more than one-half the sum agreed to be paid by Government for the transportation of the mails. Add to this, that the American line suffer disadvantages from the inexperience of its engineers and firemen, besides paying them 50 per cent. more than is paid by the English steamers; and it will hardly be necessary to add, that your memorialists cannot maintain a successful competition with them except upon the grant of such aid from our own Government, as on the basis of tonnage will correspond to that which the English admiralty extends to the Cunard line. Even on the same terms, the system of maintaining steam-packets convertible into war steamers, is recommended by its economy; for the cost to Government of laying up in ordinary such a steamer as the Baltic, or the Pacific, with interest on the outlay, deterioration, &c., would be $150,000 per annum; as may be ascertained by reference to the accounts of the steamer Mississippi.

Your memorialists therefore respectfully solicit from Congress an extension of the time in which to refund the money loaned to them by the Government, so that it may be repaid 10 per cent. annually; that amount to be deducted from the last quarterly payment in each year.

They also pray that authority may be given to the Secretary of the Navy to increase their annual compensation, having regard to the tonnage and dimensions of the steamers employed, and to the average per ton allowed to the other American lines, by their existing contracts.

Your memorialists further pray that the steamers, in time of peace, may be placed under the exclusive control of your memorialists, and be officered by them, as they apprehend that they can in no other way secure that entire responsibility which is indispensable to the perfect efficiency and safety of the service.

Your memorialists respectfully represent, that they have entered upon this enterprise with no exclusive views of commercial profit, but on national grounds, and to prevent the undisputed supremacy of the seas from falling into the hands of a rival power. The contract of your memorialists calls for ships of 2,000 tons burthen. Your memorialists were soon persuaded that with steamers of this size they could never compete successfully with the improvements and increase of the British line; and they determined to augment their bulk to about 3,000 tons. The enterprise was commenced by an incorporated company, who were the assignees of the original contractors. Of the stock but $1,100,000 was subscribed, and the difference between that and $2,500,000, the entire amount which has been expended, has been made up, with the exception of the Government advance of $385,000, mainly by the directors of the company. Any portion of this stock may be obtained at par by any one who is disposed to purchase it.

Your memorialists have little expectation of deriving pecuniary advantages from this contract, even with the solicited alterations. They are merely anxious that it should be put upon grounds which will enable them to meet the extraordinary efforts of the British steamers and the British Government and people, with an efficient and successful competition. The question has assumed a national interest. If it is understood that the American line will be sustained by the American

Government, to the extent necessary to place it on an equal footing with the British steamers, your memorialists have no doubt that, on this route, to which all the energies of Great Britain, commercial and governmental, have been directed, they will be able to achieve a complete triumph. If this aid is withheld, there is no doubt that British capital and experience, backed by the assistance of the Government, will outstrip all American competition.

Your memorialists have said that they have not entered upon this enterprise with the mere expectation of pecuniary advantages. They now declare that, if their petition should be granted by the Government, they will, at any time within six months after the passage of the act which they solicit, surrender their contract, with all its incidents and advantages, to the Secretary of the Navy, or to any individuals that may be indicated by him, on the repayment to them of the actual disbursements that have accrued in its execution. They desire merely that the monopoly which has hitherto been enjoyed may be wrested from our commercial rivals, and that the supremacy upon the ocean, which will result to the most efficient steam-marine of the world, may be at least shared with Great Britain by the United States. They believe that on this ground they will not appeal to the American Government in vain, but that all the necessary legislative aid for the accomplishment of this most desirable object will be readily granted by the representatives of the American people.

AMERICAN VIEWS.

Frow the Washington Republic, February 11.

THE SUPREMACY OF THE SEAS.

We observe that Mr. YULEE presented a few days since, in the Senate, the memorial of the contractors for the *New York and Liverpool mail steam line*, praying for some modification of their contract, with additional aid from the Government, to enable them to compete successfully with the British steamers. It is to be inferred from the memorial that, under the present arrangements, the American line cannot be sustained. The question to be solved is, whether or not the end in view is of sufficient importance to induce the extension of further assistance.

In consequence of our progress in the art of navigation, we had, a few years since, established between Europe and America the finest line of sailing packets that had ever crossed the ocean. Such was their reputation for safety and speed, that they very nearly engrossed the trade between the two continents; and especially between the United States and British islands. The CUNARD line of steamers was established for the purpose of wresting from us this material source of wealth and prosperity. So important was the object, that the British government endowed the enterprise with an immense outlay of capital, amounting, with subsequent grants, to nearly a million of dollars annually. The experiment proved highly successful. The vessels were excellent, and conducted with exceeding judgment and skill. For a period of ten years only a single vessel was lost, and the arrivals and departures attained nearly the exactitude of land conveyances. The inevitable results were, that the letter carriage, yielding thousands of dollars annually, with the transportation of bullion, passengers, and the finer and costlier kinds of merchandise, were almost wholly engrossed by the CUNARD line. Thus, not only was a large item of our best commerce taken from us, but the high road of travel and mail communication with the old world was transferred to the hands of our rivals. At the same time it was obvious that the two countries had changed positions—the Americans had lost their ascendancy, and yielded it to Great Britain.

The American, or Collins' line of mail steamers was established with a view to reverse this state of things; to recover the commerce which we had created, but which had been thus forced from us; to restore it to its natural and legitimate channels, and, in short, to assert and maintain American ascendancy where it had before existed. The enterprise attracted great attention on both sides of the Atlantic, and especially in England, where it soon became a theme of national interest and inquiry. When the American steamers got under way, and demonstrated not only our capacity to excel in beauty of model, but to contend successfully in the raee of speed, the people of the three kingdoms seemed to start as from a profound lethargy, and to cry out that the sceptre of the seas was in danger of being wrested from the accustomed grasp of Britannia.

From this time the British press teemed with articles calculated to excite the fears and rouse the pride of the nation to meet what they deemed an important crisis. The beauty, speed, and success of the American craft generally, were portrayed in vivid colors; in some cases they were even exaggerated, as a means of straining the national spirit up to the emergency. The columns of the London *Times*, *Chronicle*, *News*, &c., either lightened with omnious prophecy, or thundered with disastrous fulfilment. Many of these articles have been spread before the American public. We quote from another paper devoted to maritime affairs, and therefore a high and technical authority on this subject—the London *Nautical Standard*, January 4—for the purpose of showing, in precise terms, the train of British thought, feeling, and policy, developed by the competition of the American line of Atlantic steamers. It may be well to premise that the editorial motto of this paper is as follows: "*Whosoever commands the Sea, commands the Trade of the World; whosoever commands the trade of the World, commands the Treasures of the World, and consequently the World itself.*" It is through such spectacles that the British people read such passages as the following:

"Many times has our voice been raised, as a warning to our commercial men, to put their house in order, and not wait until it be too late. We saw coming events casting their shadows before them, and predicted that their supineness would, if not aroused in time, be their ruin. We put before them facts which were, from time to time, submitted to our consideration, not, as it has been said, with the view to frighten them, but only and solely to awaken them to their real position.

"*A people, born as it were yesterday*, has, from its own origin and intuitive powers, already succeeded in seizing a large share in the trade of the world, and, if left to itself, would in a short time have monopolized the whole commercial transatlantic shipping connexions between the old and new continents. Our warnings have been heard at the eleventh hour. We are glad and rejoice sincerely that it is so; it is not too late yet. It will now depend on the measures to be adopted if England will maintain that preponderance she has so long enjoyed, or if she will sink from the first rank in naval nations to play a secondary part.

"Now that the spirit of the British race seems to arouse from its slumbers—now that security has proved to be a snare covered with fine appearances, but deceitful and delusive to the highest degree; now that we have seen what could be done by energetic perseverance, what other nations can do, we awake to the sense of the danger that surrounds us, and wonder that we have been so long before perceiving our true situation. The whole commercial transactions of the States could not, by any stretch, provide for more than half the present tonnage afloat, or actually building. The manifest intention is to trade abroad and to supersede other nations in the carriage of goods, *to give employment to seamen, and to create by that means a mercantile navy, which, in case of war, might immediately produce a powerful manned navy, for aggressive purposes on the foreign and colonial possessions of European States.*

"But if, as we anticipate, the English nation, now awakening from her dreams of security, sees her former supremacy perilled by her long undisturbed indolence; if Englishmen, now seeing their true position and the encroachments made on their trade, resolving to shake off the trammels of old traditions or prejudices, set fairly and heartily to work; not only we do not despair of a successful issue, but, on the contrary, *we predict to them a complete restoration of those high privileges which they were once wont to consider their rights.*"

Here, then, is a glimpse at the mighty rivalry which has been excited, and is now openly avowed on the other side of the Atlantic. It is perhaps as keenly felt here, though not so vauntingly expressed. It is pushed by British writers quite beyond commercial competition to the question of armed supremacy upon the sea; and the traditional jealously and hereditary pride of England is excited by intimations that the Americans cherish the audacious scheme of usurping her birthright as legitimate Queen of the ocean!

It is of a competition thus national, and thus existing between the two great maritime powers of the earth, that the American steamers have come to be considered, in some sense, the pivot or the hinge. It was in the track of this line that England supposed she possessed high advantages, being more accustomed to the turbulent waters of the north Atlantic; more trained to battle with its tempestuous seasons; and especially more familiar with the rocky and foggy coasts at the eastern extremity of the line. It was here, also, that the British govornment had bestowed its largest and most effective pecuniary aid.

It was well reasoned that, if the Americans could beat here, they could beat anywhere or everywhere. Hence the intense interest with which the rival lines on this route are regarded. The American steamers, upon their arrival in England, have been the subjects of the most careful and critical examination. Every trip they have made has been registered, timed, scrutinized, and compared, with anxious exactitude. The decision is still pending, and the issue of the conflict is likely to depend upon the course adopted by our Government in relation to the memorial already alluded to.

If the American line shall be forced to abandon their enterprise, the rich commerce wrested from our packets by the CUNARD line will be continued in British hands. Nor will this be the end. Most of what remains on this route will also be taken away, and English merchants will reap, at our expense, the benefits of the business naturally developed under the auspices of an improved navigation. Our mails, our Government despatches, and the best means of intercourse, will be in their hands, under circumstances at all times humiliating, and, in case of national excitement or collision, of serious inconvenience or mischief.

This American Atlantic line has been viewed in this country as destined to be the beginning link in a grand chain of communication, extending through this country to California, and thence to Asia. The importance of such a line, in a national point of view, cannot be overrated. But if the Atlantic portion shall fail, the basis of this entire enterprise is annihilated. What has happened upon the Atlantic is likely to take place on the Pacific; and we shall doubtless see the richest commerce, between California and the eastern coast of Asia, engrossed by some British Cunard—triumphing by aid of government patronage over the best efforts of American enterprise. Nor are the effects likely to stop here; it is quite evident that the far-sighted British merchants and politicians do not intend it shall stop here. If the American line is crushed, the British are the victors before the world. What a moral effect must this have to discourage our commerce, and to stimulate that of the British! Must it not drive capital, courage, and enterprise from one to the other? And let it be remembered, this is not a common case of mere private competition. The government purse of Great Britain is pledged to its support; and with this mighty power added to their triumph, will not an ascendancy be gained by them which years cannot recover? It is quite evident that these things are profoundly pondered by British statesmen; and we cannot doubt that the cloud now hanging over the American line is looked to as the very threshold of that era in which they are to enter upon the success they contemplate and covet. We believe, indeed, that they calculate upon the inaction of Congress, and deem this an assurance of our failure and their success.

It is not possible to measure the effect of such British triumph upon our navigation, generally. Our steamers to Bremen and Havre, already threatened by low and losing fares from the CUNARD line, may speedily find direct British competition in the field. A race will be run for the ascendancy in the boundless trade of the Pacific now opening before the world—not on this side, in the Atlantic and Gulf of Mexico alone—but along the whole length of the western coast of our continent. Since the opening of the California mines, from Oregon to Valparaiso, a quickening impulse has been imparted to commerce. The Sandwich Islands have acquired new importance; Central America has become the theatre of gigantic schemes, for connecting two oceans, hitherto kept asunder by the landmarks of the Almighty. Peru has been awakened from its slumber of centuries, and Chili has suddenly sprung into the active area of commercial competition. A flourishing trade, with its vivifying influence, has been called into existence along a coast-line of three thousand miles, by our people and our enterprise. It belongs to us to hold the mastery of this traffic, not only that we may reap its harvest, but that we may impart to the countries with which it is connected our political and social sympathies. Yet British competition is certain to meet us here; and it is a question whether we are to contend with a people who have mastered us upon the Atlantic, and who, therefore, bring to the struggle upon the Pacific the conscious power and energy of conquerors.

Such are some of the public considerations which are forced upon the mind by the possibility that the American line of steamers may be compelled to surrender. It is impossible to consider it as a mere question of individual capital and private enterprise. Both Britain and the United States have made the competing lines, to some extent, national, by direct government patronage; the vessels of both are, contingently, government ships, and that, too, for naval purposes. Even if we treat the American line as a private interest, and refuse to sustain it on that ground, we leave it to be overborne by the national purse and policy of Great Britain, and in a contest which involves our own national interests to the extent of uncounted millions.

To these general views it may be well to add a few particular facts as to the American line. Within the short compass of three years, this company has built and put into operation four steamships, of an aggregate burden of 11,000 tons. The vessels are acknowledged to be the finest models that ever floated. Their passages are among the shortest ever known. They have met with neither hindrance nor delay, except in the winter passages; here, a want of experience has caused some irregularities, which are, however, now provided against. One vessel is missing, and her fate being unknown, she cannot be made the basis of calculation here. It may be said, in general, that the American line has at least demonstrated our capacity to sustain a successful and triumphant competition with the British line, and thus to maintain the credit of our navigation before the world.

In the progress of this enterprise the American company have met with unexpected difficulties. It has been necessary to construct machinery, and to devise, make, or import tools of larger dimensions and more massive form than existed in the country before; all of which may hereafter be useful, if not essential, in the event of war. The qualities of the various kinds of iron have been tested and the best ascertained; thus enabling future machinists to construct engines that may be relied upon for the severest ocean service. They have, as above suggested, acquired by experience a knowledge of the peculiar difficulties of winter steam navigation upon the north Atlantic, and ascertained the means of countervailing them. They have thus, at great expense, made extensive experiments, and largely advanced the knowledge and means essential to success in steam navigation.

Other difficulties have been experienced which are more annoying. "The contest," says the Philadelphia North American, "is not a fair one, and, so far as the steamships are concerned, the rivalry is conducted on the side of the British on such principles, and with a resort to such expedients to secure the advantage, as show the importance attached by them to the struggle, and their determination to be victors at every hazard and at any cost. In a commercial aspect, the rivalry has been pursued by them in a pitiful, huckstering spirit, which has infected the press, the public, the very Government, as well as those directly interested in the British ships. A great many sly means have been used to prejudice the character of the American ships by the circulation of unfounded rumors of defective machinery, accidents, &c.; the post office authorities threw, as long as they decently could, the weight of their official influence against the American ships; and the immediate managers of the English lines have always been ready with the small device of reduced freights to drive away shippers."

A few days since, in an article on this subject, we made statements analagous to these. They were questioned by the *Albion, a British colonial gazette*, published at New York, and one relating to the unfairness of the British press was somewhat flatly denied. We did not allude to open statements; for we were fully aware that, in general, the American steamers have been praised by the London papers. We had in view such insidious paragraphs as the following from the Liverpool journal of October 12: "*The Atlantic is under examination at New York, and the Arctic is to take her place.*" Both statements were utterly without foundation, and could only have been the work of invention; the sinister import is too obvious to leave a doubt on the subject. If the New York *Albion* will consult its Liverpool namesake for the last six months, we are assured it will find abundance of similar statements and rumors, fully bearing out our assertions. The Latin quotation of the *Albion*, with its context, importing that the misfortunes of the Collins' line had drawn us into an "ebullition of spite," were too natural and national to provoke a reply. The material parts of our article are confirmed by the above extract from the *North American*, and, indeed, by the small criticims of the *Albion* itself; for surely it would not have confined itself to fishing for minnows, if more substantial sport had been at hand.

We have been drawn into a much more extended notice of this subject than we intended. We cannot conclude, however, without observing, that it seems to us that a more inopportune occasion could hardly be selected than the present for resting upon any half-way and inadequate measures of competition. Nothing is more apparent than that wise policy, and the feeling of the people demand a national spirit, tone, and action on the part of the Government. No State document ever received a more hearty response from the people than Mr. WEBSTER's late letter to the Austrian minister; and we believe that the encouragement of no branch of national interest on the part of Congress would be more heartily approved throughout the country, than that which aims at our maritime independence of Great Britain. Our past experience and past history have taught us all to regard this as linked alike with individual prosperity and national power, peace, and renown.

From the Philadelphia North American.

THE EMPIRE OF THE SEAS.

The rapid growth of the American steam marine—the indications furnished by at least the summer passages of the New York steamships across the Atlantic—in connexion with the proof, seen in the well known voyage of the Oriental from Hong Kong to London, of the superiority of American over British sailing vessels, have produced no little alarm among the patriots of the fast-anchored isle, who dread the transference of the empire of the seas, so long maintained by England against the world, to the hands of their enterprising cousins of the new world. It is very certain that a struggle for commercial supremacy is going, and has long been going, on between the two countries; and it is, perhaps, also certain that the victory would be speedily acquired by American energies over British pride and British capital, were those energies properly fostered by Government, and not exposed to suffer, as they do, from the continual discouragements of an unfriendly and unnatural revenue system.

The contest is not a fair one; and, so far as the steamships are concerned, the rivalry is conducted on the side of the British on such principles, and with a resort to such expedients to secure the advantage, as show the importance attached by them to the struggle, and their determination to be victors at every hazard and at any cost. In a commercial aspect, the rivalry has been pursued by them in a pitiful, huckstering spirit, which has infected the press, the public, the very Government, as well as those directly interested in the British ships. A great many sly means have been used to prejudice the character of the American ships by the circulation of unfounded rumors of defective machinery, accidents, &c.; the post office authorities threw, as long as they decently could, the weight of their official influence against the American ships; and the immediate managers of the English lines have always been ready with the small device of reduced freights to drive away shippers. The following extract from a speech by Mr. Butler King, of Georgia, delivered in the House of Representatives as far back as July 19, 1848, will be remembered as showing that this latter game was resorted to, at that early period, against the first American steamer which visited Liverpool:

"In the discussions which have been occasioned by the appropriations to meet the contracts for this mail service, it has been argued that it is quite unnecessary for the Government to contribute in any degree to sustain it; that private enterprise, if left untrammelled 'by Government schemes and legal enactments,' would sustain itself against all foreign competition. To show the fallacy of this reasoning, it is only necessary to state a few facts connected with the recent voyage of the steamer 'United States' to Liverpool. The price of freight from Liverpool to New York, as established by the Cunard line, is £7 sterling per ton, and the price of passage £30 per head. While the United States was in the dock at Liverpool, the agents of the Cunard line, to prevent freight and passengers going in her, reduced the price of freight to £4 per ton by the 'Hibernia,' and to £2 1s. by the 'Niagara,' and they offered to take passengers as low as £12 per head.

"It was announced at the same time, in Harnden's Liverpool circular, that the old rates would be resumed immediately after the departure of the American ship. The British line, sustained by the Government, was enabled to adopt this course with impunity in competition with a ship sustained by individual enterprise alone; and it must, I suppose, be admitted that our citizens, if not aided in undertakings of this sort by their own Government, would be quite incapable of competing for any length of time with so powerful an opposition. This being the case, it must be apparent to any one who will investigate the subject that, in a very short time, the most valuable portion of our carrying trade would pass into the bottoms of these British mail packets."

The more recent case of the Franklin will not be forgotten, where the similar artifice was attempted—to the honor of the French shippers, without any success—of offering to take freight from Havre to New York at ten dollars a ton, against the thirty dollars or upwards, the regular rates, asked by the owners of the Franklin.

In our efforts to place American steam navigation on a safe footing, we shall, doubtless, have to contend with this sort of policy, and with all the interested prejudices of our English rivals—who have the merit of sticking by each other in every contest, even when justice is not altogether on their side—until we have overcome both, as we shall ultimately do. In the mean while, the moral that lies at the bottom of the controversy should not be overlooked. In the British view, national safety is interwoven with the idea of marine supremacy. Every steam packet now built in England is a steam-frigate added to the British navy. Every American steam packet should be regarded as a similar addition to the American navy. Every thing should be done by us to stimulate the increase of American steam ships, and to direct their construction so as to render them capable of being employed, whenever necessary, as arms of the national defence.

From the Washington Republic.

THE SUPPLY OF FUEL TO THE COLLINS LINE OF STEAMERS.

Owing to the concurrence of two of the steamers of the Collins line recently running short of coal, and the painful anxiety which is felt respecting the absence of a third, rumors prejudicial to the owners and managers of the line have crept into circulation. We find in the New York *Herald* a communication from an engineer, which corrects some of these erroneous reports, and furnishes some explanation of the reasons which caused the Baltic and Arctic to put into Provincetown and Halifax to replenish their fuel. We presume that every American feels a proper pride in the reputation which our steamers have acquired for speed, and a solicitude that their management should also be unexcelled. Renewed efforts were necessary to win us the palm for the one, and untiring energy and diligence will assuredly never be wanting to secure us the meed for the other.

It is only those who fail to profit by experience who are justly censurable for neglect. None of the Collins line of steamers, we are informed, have ever put to sea without an abundant supply of coal; but that supply has proved insufficient in two instances, from a misapprehension which could only be corrected by long observation and scientific inquiry. This misapprehension was in largely increasing the fuel on encountering a gale, the reverse of which, it appears, is the proper practice, and that which is pursued by the British steamers. Sir Edward Belcher, of the British royal navy, has communicated the fact that, when steamers are heading a gale, it is necessary to check the draft in order to preserve or increase the heat, because experience, he says, has demonstrated that the immense volume of cold air which is poured into the furnaces at such a time, with an open draft, though it increases the combustion of the coal, yet chills the gases, and prevents the generation of an amount of heat which could be obtained from a more moderate fire with the draft partially cut off. Moreover, it is ascertained that in certain cases even an increased physical momentum of the vessel is a positive disadvantage, inasmuch as by it the vessel is driven with such force, when descending a wave into the recurring wave, that her average speed is greatly diminished. We have no doubt the Collins line will be prompt to avail itself of these and other valuable suggestions which are derived from experience; while, at the same time, it is plain that the owner and directors should be exculpated from all criminal intent or indifference in the matter referred to. We subjoin the communication of the *Herald*:

" *The Collins line of steamers.*—The late passages of these steamers being such as to induce, with the public at large, impressions unfavorable to the capacities of these vessels for western passages in the winter season, it is but justice to Mr. Collins, to the directors of this line, and to the American public, who have manifested so much interest and satisfaction in the hitherto performances of the pioneers of this line, that they should be set aright as to the cause which has led to the late interruptions in the homeward trips of the 'Baltic' and 'Arctic.'

" All of the vessels of this line consume fuel, *pro rata* for the power of their engines, in a less quantity than any marine steamers yet constructed in any country; and they also have capacity for the stowage of it, commensurate with their consumption, in a proportion greater than has ever yet been attained or allotted to a steamer for a like length of route. Their deficiency, then, has not arisen from the causes that have compelled other Liverpool or European steamers in western passages to put into Halifax, viz., undue consumption and insufficient capacity; but it has arisen from an undue estimate of the severity and difficulties of western passages at this season, and too much preference being given to freight; added to which there was an error in the manner of working the furnaces of the Baltic, which was not discovered until the consumption of coal had been such as to compel her to put in for a supply. Probably the same error has been fallen into with the management of the boilers of the Arctic.

"There is another difficulty that these steamers, in common with all American steamers, are subjected to, and that is, the inexperience of their firemen. The importance of this point is one that cannot be appreciated by the public; but it is one pregnant with more loss of time and waste of fuel than I dare venture to assert with any confidence of its general credit. It has been said, and with truth, too, by those connected with the Cunard line, 'Give us your vessels and we will beat you a day;' and they might have added, and save ten tons of coal per day.

"Of the capacities of these vessels I am as cognizant as an intimate knowledge of the mechanical details of all of them, and a witness of the performance at sea (and in heavy weather, too) of one of them, can make me, and I have the fullest conviction of their unsurpassed qualities in speed and endurance. The recurrence of the error which has led to the Baltic and Arctic running short of fuel has already been guarded against, and they will assume and maintain the position they have the elements for, and which is one that will meet the fullest wishes of the country which has produced them.

"Of the Atlantic, a knowledge of her capacities as a sea boat, and of her endurance as a structure, induces the opinion that, having become short of fuel, or her engines, probably her wheels, having failed her, she had been compelled to put back when near to this coast, and had not arrived in season to communicate with the Arctic, prior to the sailing of this vessel on the 11th instant. If, however, neither of these causes has led to her non-arrival here, the failure is not from weakness, or insufficient sea-going qualities, but is one arising from causes not confined to this line, or American steam navigation.

"ENGINEER."

From the Washington Republic, January 28.

THE COLLINS AND CUNARD LINES.

From the commencement of CUNARD's line, as every body knows, it was favored by our whole country. New York and Boston vied with each other, at the very outset, in offering it civilities and facilities. When the first of the line arrived at Boston, the occasion was celebrated by high festivities, in which the city authorities and leading men of the State participated. The officers were fêted and feasted, and CUNARD himself became the hero of the day. From that time to this the American feeling toward the CUNRAD line has been generous—not to say magnanimous. For the first five or six years a series of untoward accidents occurred, crippling several of the vessels, and delaying or intering their passages. One of them—the Columbia—was lost on her way from Boston to Halifax, and the large number of passengers escaped a watery grave, almost by miracle. But in all these cases no spirit of hypercriticism was manifested here; on the contrary, excuse and apology overlooked every accident, and explained away every failure.

When COLLINS's line commenced operations this state of things still continued, the rivalry being regarded here mainly as to its tendency to improve steam navigation. If our national pride led us to wish for the triumph of the American steamers, every man in the country would have looked with disdain upon any attempt, on our part, to gain an advantage not due to superiority in skill, courage, or energy. But how has this liberal spirit been met in England? It is now well known that a series of tricks has been resorted to there, for the purpose of cutting off the patronage of the COLLINS steamers, and diverting it to the Royal Mail line. This is done by false statements in the newspapers, and injurious rumors spread over the country in various ways. Some months since, when the passengers were about to set out from Paris for Liverpool, to embark in the Pacific, a story, utterly without foundation, was put in circulation, that she had broken her bed-plate. The passengers, deceived by this story, of course waited a few days, and took their departure in the CUNARD steamer, which followed. Insidious statements, of a similiar kind, have frequently been set afloat at the critical moments when the American vessels were about to depart; and we are informed that some of these have been traced to interested parties. That such is their origin, the times at which they appear, and the system with they are propagated, leave little room to doubt. The general feeling of local interest, and the national prejudice in England, give these rumors an abiding, not to say fatal, effect. Well knowing that the reputation of a ship, in which men risk their lives and their property, is of the most delicate character, and may be ruined by the lightest breath of rumor, the operators in this case have found it both convenient and easy to poison the railways and thoroughfares of England with their slanders. A gentleman interested in the COLLINS line, travelling in England a short time since, was told by an intelligent stranger whom he met in one of the cars, that the American steamers were built of green timber, and were already falling to pieces. Another gentleman, being lately in London, was kindly and gratuitously advised by a bank clerk—a total stranger—not to take passage in any American steamer, as they were universally considered unsafe!

Such is a specimen of the artifices now practised in England against the COLLINS steamers. The Bremen and Havre lines have been less the objects of this species of warfare, because they are less direct competitors of the CUNARD ships. Yet, as the Franklin was recently taking in her freight at Havre, in order to strike a fatal blow at her success, the CUNARD line announced that they would take freight from that port to New York for ten dollars a ton, which was about one-third of ehafair rate. This was done while the shippers from Liverpool were held to the ordinary prices of thirty or thirty-five dollars a ton. We rejoice to say that the agents of the Franklin disdained to enter into this corrupting competition, and even the shippers at Havre scorned the bribe. The Franklin came with a full freight, at regular prices, leaving the CUNARD line fully exposed before the world, as to the spirit with which it is conducted, and that too without even the solace of success.

We note these facts, not for the purpose of provoking retaliation in kind, for we hope and trust the Americans will never descend to this unworthy species of warfare. We notice it only to keep our countrymen apprised of the character of those with whom we have to deal in the impending competition, and, indeed, in every competition with British agents.

Though we have no doubt of the final issue of this rivalry in steam navigation, we conceive it proper to make a few suggestions, which may moderate our expectations of immediate supremacy. It must be remembered, that, from the beginning, steam navigation was mainly employed by us upon our rivers. These, hundreds or thousands of miles in length, traversing the very depths of the country, naturally became the theatre of our first triumphs in this noble discovery. It was glory enough that we were able to convert these into the great thoroughfares of travel and trade, ere yet the old world was fully awake to the new era which had begun. Our steamboats, thus confined to shallow waters and influenced by the spirit of the country, soon became subject to a keen competition for speed. The swiftest boat was, of course, deemed the best. All the genius of our artisans was bent to this species of excellence, and accordingly we soon led the world in the celerity of our steamers. Our boats, in their very models, suggested by their length and lightness the predominant purpose of their construction. The arrow in its flight, or the outstretched swan skimming the wave, were favorite images associated with our steamers, and gave name to some of the most popular and successful boats.

It is true, indeed, that our river navigation—at first a matter of thrift and convenience—speedily became also a matter of luxury. While sailing up or down the Hudson, the Ohio, or the Mississippi, some of the finest scenery in the world was added to the advantage of unrivalled speed in the passage. Thus by degrees our steamers were converted into floating palaces, with the sumptuous decorations of architecture, and the gustful allurements of the table. All this, however, was rather incidental, the main idea of excelling in speed still continuing to prevail.

It was just the reverse in Great Britain. Here the most renowned rivers are but little larger than our mill-streams. Her steamers were to traverse the turbulent waters, which never cease to foam and thunder around her rocky coasts. It was from the very beginning a battle of might with might—of human will and strength against the wonted mastery of the deep. It was not, as in the old navigation, a contest in which the wind was seduced into coquetry with the sea—the trick of the rudder teaching the ship to glide over and avoid, rather than meet, the shock of the waves. A new power, dug by man's arm from the bowels of the earth, and linked with iron by man's invention, was to impel the vessel in the very teeth of the wind, and against the very breast of the embattled billows. It was a strife worthy of the descendants of the Sea-Kings of other days. In a superstitious age of the world it would have been regarded as an impious waging of war upon the gods. How would these things have rung in the sonorous numbers of the Father of Poetry?

Yet such was Britain's apprenticeship in steam navigation. While the motto of our steamers was *go ahead*, her's was of necessity *go sure*. And thus for five and twenty years the people of the British islands have been trained in one set of ideas regarding steam navigation, and we in another; and what is specially pertinent to the purpose of this article, for this period of time, she has been establishing foundries, erecting ship-yards, building engines, and rearing practical engineers, exactly suited to meet us, and perhaps defeat us, in the contest which has now begun, as to superiority in one line of ocean steam navigation.

Nor is this superior experience, in navigating the turbulent waters of the northern seas, the only advantage in the hands of our rivals. Her immense mineral resources, especially her inexhaustible beds of iron and coal, lying contiguous to each other, and near to navigable waters, with the low price of labor by which these are made cheap and abundant at any required port, place a power in her hands decisive of a contest which is not met and sustained by corresponding or countervailing advantages, added to indomitable perseverance.

And to all this we must add, that John Bull's long and heavy purse is put at the disposal of our British competitors. As the haughty Brennus, while Rome hesitated about the golden ransom she was to pay, put his sword in the scale, exclaiming, "wo to the conquered;" so Britain casts the might of her money into the issue. The government aid given by England to the CUNARD line is twice or thrice that bestowed by Congress upon the COLLINS steamers; and to what she has given she stands ready to add more. The applicants need not go to Parliament; it is only necessary to satisfy the Board of Trade to insure additional millions for this object. An English gentleman, recently discussing the subject, adduced this fact as insuring the final triumph of the CUNARD line, particularly as he counted upon the supposed reluctance of an American Congress to grant money to this and kindred objects!

Yet, fully appreciating all these advantages on the side of the British steamers, we have no fear as to the result. In river steamers we surpass all other nations; in ocean steam navigation, in the milder latitudes, we are also without a rival. No other ships can compare with our lines to the south, to the Gulf of Mexico, and from Panama to San Francisco. In summer navigation of the northern Atlantic, Collins' line is at least equal to Cunard's; if there be an advantage it is on our side. We now speak only of speed; in comfort to passengers, in taste and general arrangement, we have an admitted superiority. In the winter navigation—the only point in which our inferiority can be pretended—two of COLLINS' line have run short of coal, owing doubtless to a want of experience as to the use of it on the part of the engineers. For the first eight years the CUNARD line stopped at Halifax, and always took in coal, which is only what these two ships have done, each in one instance. Even such accidents will not be likely to occur, after this experience.

We have little space in which to consider the aspect which this question of superiority in steam navigation bears upon the prospects of our own country and Great Britain. Of the six hundred ships of war forming the present British navy, about one hundred are steamers, bearing the titles of Adder, Avenger, Basilisk, Bloodhound, Bulldog, Firebrand, Fury, Goliah, Spitfire, Terrible, Viper, Vixen, Volcano, &c. To this euphoneous list must be added her mail steamers. Such a force is doubtless sufficient to master the other navies of Europe; and thus, if America were out of the way, Britannia might still assert and sing her dominion of the waves.

That in this condition of things John Bull is chewing the cud of bitter fancies there can be no doubt. We regret to see, in the British press, a train of ideas and suggestions which, if indulged, may again crimson the ocean with the blood of the two kindred nations. The time is past when mankind will endure the idea of an iron Gibraltar steaming over the world, and making every flag that flies the play thing of Britain's iron will. This notion of supremacy of the seas—of triumph on the one hand and humiliation on the other—should never go beyond commercial rivalry. And it should be the effort of all good men to divest this, as far as possible, of any embittering tendency. Yet it is certain, that by the manner in which this subject is discussed by leading papers in England, that statesmen there are looking beyond commercial superiority to their ancient maritime dominion; and it is equally clear, that in the greedy pursuit of this object, the people of England are returning evil for good toward this country, in respect to the existing competition. The British steamers to our own ports have met with universal favor; our steamers to British ports have been the objects, and to some extent the victims, of conspiracies, to which the press have been, in certain instances, a party!

☞These are but a small portion of the articles which have appeared in the American papers, on this subject, concurring in and enforcing these views. It may be added here, that it appears from parliamentary documents, that the CUNARD line now returns to the British Government, in the proceeds of the mails, the full amount of the sum advanced to them, which is about £185,000 annually. Thus it operates only as a loan. Were the American Liverpool line so far encouraged by our Government as to put it on a level with the other American lines, it is believed the operation would be the same as above stated in respect to the CUNARD line; that is, the product of the mails would probably restore to the Government the full amount of its advances.

BRITISH VIEWS.

From the London Daily News, October 11.

THE SUPREMACY OF THE SEAS—COLLINS AND CUNARD.

Racing is the great passion of the Englishman. Horse-racing, boat-racing, foot-racing, donkey-racing; no kind of racing comes amiss to him. Wherever the Englishman goes he must have his races. There are regular boat-races at the Cook's strait settlements, in New-Zeland, and there is a race-course at Sierra Leone.

A race is even now "coming off," on which England has a stake of terrible magnitude. We allude to that race of an indefinite number of heats, now running on the Atlantic, by CUNARD's and COLLINS' ocean steamers. The stake is neither more nor less than the ascendancy on the seas. We use the word not in a silly and obsolete sense of those who used to dream of any one nation asserting by force of arms a mastery in maritime affairs over all other nations. Henceforth there can be no sovereign nation; the great community of nations is and must continue a republic. But even in republics there are individuals who possess more wealth, more power than others. England is still the first citizen of the community of nations; the flag of England is still the foremost on the ocean. If England loses the Cunard and Collins race, it will be an event of bad omen for her maritime pre-eminence. French pageants at Cherbourg, Russian demonstrations on the Baltic, can only alarm old women in and out of petticoats. Pre-eminence at sea must belong to the nation which possesses the most numerous and best appointed mercantile marine, and the most important branch of the country's mercantile marine will ere long be its ocean steamers. If it be true that an American steamer has beaten our fastest and finest vessels on an Atlantic voyage, it is high time that we had a more searching inquiry into the state of our ocean steam communication than was vouchsafed by Mr. Henley's committee.

According to the New York accounts, the American ocean steamer Pacific made her last voyage from Liverpool to New York in 10 days 4¾ hours from wharf to wharf. We suspect the time was a little longer. A writer in yesterday's *Times* states, that the Pacific left Liverpool at 2 p. m. on the 11th September. The New York papers state that it reached that city at 5h. 45m. p. m. on the 21st ult. Add 4h. 45m. for the difference of the time occasioned by difference of longitude, and we have 10 days 8½ hours for the length of the passage.

The English ocean steamer Asia is said to have made her last homeward voyage in 10 days 7 hours. Allowance must, however, be made for the greater speed with which, owing to the set of the currents, the voyage from America to England is accomplished, than the voyage from England to America. The Asia's outward voyage to New York was accomplished in 10 days 11 hours 36 minutes, mean steaming time. From this, we are told, must be deducted 5 hours for the detour by

Halifax. But this allowance is in excess; the increased distance is not the only element to be considered; the less resistance from oceanic currents on the Halifax route ought also to be taken into account.

On the whole we are disposed to admit that the Pacific, not the Asia, has made the quickest passage yet made between Liverpool and New York. It is, however, a neck and neck affair. In July last the American ocean steamer Atlantic made the voyage from New York to Liverpool in ten days, eight hours, twenty minutes, only one hour twenty minutes in excess of the time taken by the Asia.

We are anxious to state the facts correctly, for there is an evident and not unnatural straining on the part both of English and Americans to make out the best case for their respective steamers. Even on the assumption that the victory is still doubtful, the result cannot be very gratifying to onr national pride. CUNARD's company have had ten years' practice; the first experiment in Atlantic steam navigation, on the part of the Americans, was made last year by the New York and Bremen steamers. The Pacific and Atlantic are the first steamers launched by the COLLINS' company. Yet one of these trial ships, if it have not beaten, has equalled the matured production of CUNARD's company. Is there any thing in the history of our ocean steam navigation that can account for this?

Some ten years back, Government unable or unwilling to carry the mails across the Atlantic, granted a contract to Mr. Samuel Cunard, which that fortunate gentleman is understood to have sold at a great premium to a Glasgow company for the conveyance by steam-vessels of her Majesty's mails between Liverpool, Halifax, and Boston. In 1846 this contract was renewed for ten years from the 1st of January, 1848; and, in expectation of the American competition which has since arisen, leave was given to omit Halifax, and make the voyage direct from Liverpool to New York. Both the original contract and its extension were given without any competition. The owners of the Great Western and other steam-vessels, who had risked their money in establishing the practicability of making the Atlantic voyage, were unceremoniously brushed aside, and the contractor has had a virtual monopoly of the steam communication between the United States and this country for the last ten years. For this service the country pays 140,000*l*. per annum.

Following the example of the English government, the United States granted in 1848, to a New York company, a contract for carrying the mails to Liverpool; and their two first vessels, the Atlantic and Pacific, made their appearance this year, to be followed next spring by the Arctic and the Baltic. The CUNARD company, thus put on their mettle, constructed the Asia and the Africa, which were also placed on the station this year. The result of the contest, as far as it has been carried, is stated above.

"We are ten years before you in ship-building," said a Yankee skipper, the other day; "and ten years behind you in machinery; in five years more we will be ahead of you in both." To prove JONATHAN wrong we shall have to get up some competition at home, and not wait to be taught the old lesson that there is no such thing in nature as an improving monopoly.

Cunard's Company commenced with vessels of 1,100 tons, and engines of 350 horse-power. They have, step by step, reached 2,300 tons and 900 horse-power. But the size and power are the only things changed; the model has remained the same. The Asia, of 2,300 tons, is an enlarged edition of the Britannia of 1,100 tons, and goes bowling down the Mersey, carrying a sea before her enough to swamp a revenue cruiser.

The American steamers are of larger tonnage and less power than the Asia and Africa, but of exquisite model. They are "ten years ahead" of the Asia and Africa, as far as the hulls are concerned, and as far behind in the engines. They slip down the Mersey with scarce a ripple at the bow, dividing the water like a Gravesend steamer. In accommodation, ventilation, and general arrangement, the American vessels are far superior to anything that has been before seen in this country.

It will doubtless be said that we attach too much importance to the success of our transatlantic cousins. We shall be told that "one swallow does not make a summer; one extraordinary passage is not a fair criterion." We shall be advised to wait for a twelvemonth before we give an opinion. In spite, however, of these and other wise saws that may be poured out, we confess that to us the voyages of the Atlantic and the Pacific look like "the handwriting on the wall" to our rulers, which it behooves them to lay to heart.

From the London Atheneum, Jan. 4.

THE GREAT NATIONAL CONTEST.

In an age like this, when the real rivalries and contests of nations are carried on, not so much by regiments and frigates, as by means of the shuttle, the railway, and the steamboat—it is curious and important to note the progress of different countries in those practical arts and sciences which more immediately promote these friendly national contests.

European statesmen have all watched with wonder, and not a few of them with alarm, the tremendous accession of power which the rapid development of railways, telegraphs, and steam navigation in the United States has given to the people of North America, an accession of political and material influence in the affairs of the world, which seems to stand in almost startling disproportion to the mere weight of the masses of population. The Brazils, by nature far richer than the northern States in all the raw materials of power, have no more voice in determining the direction of great historical events than a petty German or Italian principality. Belgium, covered with railways, anp dotted with manufactories, has already more active influence in Europe than the once powerful and magnificent kingdom of Spain. Science multiplies the resources of nations in an extraordinary degree; and older games of ambition are so far gone out of modern fashion, that statesmen, with the true instincts of the future about them, care less and less about drilling regiments, and more and more about promoting science.

The trials of strength in this noble contest lie at present chiefly between the two great divisions of the Anglo-Saxon race. England, by insular position, and America by her geographical remoteness, stand tolerably free from the wear of intellect and waste of material means which are daily seen in the political struggles of continental Europe; and they are, as regards each other, therefore, on equal and fair terms of competition. With the shuttle England might be conquered, even while her hearts of oak defied the world. A French army on the coast of Devonshire or Kent might prove a passing evil ; but a combination of natural and mechanical advantages secured to the workshops of the United States, would be utter and irretrievable ruin. Thus far, the shuttle of Manchester beats the shuttle of Lowell; hitherto, the steam vessel of Liverpool has outsped that of New York.

But the forces are so nearly matched as to lead all the charm of an uncertain issue to the struggle. Especially is this the case with the ocean steamers. In river, lake, and coast navigation, America has long carried away the palm of victory. The boats on the Rhine, the Elbe, the Clyde, the Thames, and the Scheldt, are not for a moment to be compared with the "floating palaces" on the Hudson, the Delaware, and the Potomac, either for rate of sailing or for magnificence of fitting up. We have been credibly told of vessels steaming down the Mississippi at the rate of twenty-five miles an hour! But in ocean navigation, longer practice and equal enterprise still keep us slightly ahead of our energetic descendants. We are proud of our rivals—as they are proud of our rivalry. To the general reader at home, it is next to impossible to convey an adequate idea of the interest which the contests between the English and American mails excite in Boston, New York, and Philadelphia. Each run is carefully noted and compared ; fears are excited, hopes raised, by every voyage; and half a dozen hours in the length of a trip of three thousand miles is thought a considerable variation.

The struggle for mastery at this moment lies between the English mail Asia and the American mail Atlantic; and the recent voyage of the Asia was the quickest ever yet performed. This passage from New York to Liverpool was made in ten days four hours and five minutes, being four hours and fifteen minutes less than the best voyage eastward made by the Atlantic. The New Yorkers are building still more powerful vessels for this line of service. The prize is a great one. The fleetest vessels must carry out letters, orders, news, Government despatches; and, having the prestige of scientific excellence and success, will generally command a choice of the passenger traffic. In this rivalry the Americans possess a great advantage over us, in being less fettered in their action by Government jobbing and monopoly.

From the Halifax (N. S.) Chronicle.

THE UNITED STATES MAIL STEAMER ARCTIC.

This magnificent ocean steamship arrived in our harbor yesterday morning, after a very boisterous passage of thirteen days from the Mersey. She left Liverpool on the 11th inst., with thirty-five passengers, a large and valuable freight, and had on board when starting about one thousand tons of coal. The captain finding the supply of fuel decreasing rapidly, very prudently bore up for this port. This adds one more to the thousand and one proofs of the desirableness of making Halifax harbor, if not a terminus, at least an intermediate packet station. In common with many other citizens, we had the pleasure of visiting this, really splendid ship yesterday. We are happy to bear testimony to the civility and attention extended by the Arctic's officers to all who enjoyed the privilege. Nothing can possibly surpass the magnificence of this the first of the Collins line, that has yet paid us a visit. So many descriptions of these vessels have already been published, by those infinitely more competent than us, that any recapitulation would be altogether superfluous. Every thing on board, including the mammoth engines, is in the most perfect order. The interior arrangements of the Arctic far, very far, surpass in elegance any thing of the kind previously seen in Halifax.

SPEECH

OF THE

HON. J. W. MILLER,

OF NEW JERSEY,

ON

AMERICAN MAIL STEAMERS.

DELIVERED

IN THE SENATE OF THE UNITED STATES,

APRIL 22, 1852.

"That striking simile of England's military power, 'the roll of her drum is heard from the rising to the setting of the sun,' will be changed. War and conquest will give way to peace and commerce, and the ring of the ocean steamer's bell will be heard on every sea, and along every coast, bell pealing to bell, the world round."

WASHINGTON:
PRINTED BY JOHN T. TOWERS.
1852.

SPEECH

OF THE

HON. J. W. MILLER,

OF NEW JERSEY,

IN

FAVOR OF SUSTAINING THE COLLINS LINE OF AMERICAN MAIL STEAMERS.

DELIVERED IN THE SENATE OF THE UNITED STATES, APRIL 22, 1852.

WASHINGTON:
PRINTED BY JNO. T. TOWERS.
1852.

SPEECH.

The Senate resumed the consideration of the bill to supply deficiencies in the appropriations for the service of the fiscal year ending June 30, 1852. The following amendment being under consideration: "For additional compensation for increasing the transportation of the United States mail between New York and Liverpool, in the Collins line of steamers, to twenty-six trips per annum, at such times as shall be directed by the Postmaster General, and in conformtty to his last annual report to Congress, and his letter of the fifteenth of November last to Secretary of the Navy, commencing said increased service on the first of January, eighteen hundred and fifty two, at the rate of thirty-three thousand dollars per trip, in lieu of the present allowance, the sum of two hundred and thirty-six thousand five hundred dollars."

Mr. MILLER said: Mr. President, I was one of the majority of the Committee on Finance which agreed to report this amendment. The subject had been recommended to Congress by the head of one of the departments, and a general estimate made, which was produced before the committee by the honorable Senator from California, (Mr. GWIN.) The question presented by the amendment I considered to be one of very high importance to the country; in which not only the parties to this contract, but many of the great interests of the country are concerned. In the year 1849, a contract was entered into by this Government, through the Navy Department, with Mr. Collins and others, to build a certain number of mail ocean steamers, giving a description of their general power and capicity, and specifying the purposes for which they were to be used. By that contract the steamers were to perform twenty trips a year—that is, monthly trips during four months of the year, and semi-monthly trips during eight months of the year; and for which service he was to receive the sum of $385,000.

The objects which the Government and Congress had in view in entering into this contract were of a national character. They were, in the first place, to secure the speedy and cheap transportation of letters to and from this country to Europe.

In the second place, the Government desired to have built ocean steamers of sufficient power and capacity that they might, in case of an emergency, be employed by the Government in war. Other collateral and public objects were taken into consideration—such as the transportation of passengers, of light articles of freight, and specie—which at that time were under the control of English steamers. These were the objects which induced Congress to pass the law authorizing the contract.

Now, Mr. President, I intend to show, in the remarks which I shall make on this occasion, that all these national objects have been accomplished; that Collins & Co. have built four ocean steamers of great power and superior speed; that they are transporting the foreign mails in less time than was ever accomplished before; that the Government may at any time, in case of an emergency, command the service of four of the most splendid steamers that were ever built, surpassing in speed, in power, and in tonnage any ships of the kind now afloat; that by means of the establishment of the American line we now successfully compete with and even surpass in speed its great English rival, the Cunard line; that the American people now enjoy all those great advantages which were contemplated by Congress at the time the contract was made, and that every obligation on the part of the contractors has been faithfully performed by them. But, sir, in performing this great enterprise, so advantageous to the country, the contractors have sustained great losses. They state their loss during the last year to be $338,574—in other words, that in every trip which they performed during the last year they lost $16,928 79.

Sometime during the last autumn, the Cunard line of steamers having been ordered up to weekly service the year round, the Postmaster General deemed it his duty to direct Mr. Collins to increase the trips of his line from twenty to twenty-six per year, and to commence on the first of January last, with assurances of additional compensation to be made by Congress.

This arrangement appears by the letters of the Postmaster General and the Secretary of the Navy, which I will read:

Post Office Department, *November* 15, 1851.

Sir: By their contract, the proprietors of the Collins line of steamers between New York and Liverpool, as you are aware, are required to perform only twenty voyages per annum—that is, monthly trips during four months, and semi monthly trips eight months, of each year. In alternating, as at present, with the steamers of the Cunard line, we are informed by Mr. Collins that, by the first of January next, his steamers will have made seventeen trips—leaving only three voyages to be performed from the 1st January to the 27th April, the end of the contract year.

The Cunard line has now been ordered up to weekly service the year round; and deeming it highly important, therefore, that the trips on the Collins line should be increased from twenty to twenty-six a year, I have already given Mr. Collins the assurance that if he shall see fit to run the necessary additional trips, to alternate, as at present, with the British lines through the year, and will look to Congress for compensation, I will recommend to Congress the allowance of *pro rata* or such additional pay therefor as shall be considered fair and proper under the circumstances.

It cannot be doubted that it is for the interest of the United States to afford such aid to the Collins line as will enable it to compete successfully with the British lines running in connexion therewith; and I beg leave to call your attention to the subject, in the hope that you will unite with me in such recommendation to Congress as will secure the increase of the service of the Collins line from twenty to twenty-six trips a year as a permanent arrangement.

I have the honor to be, very respectfully, your obedient servant,

N. K. HALL,
Postmaster General.

Hon. W. A. Graham, *Secretary of the Navy.*

NAVY DEPARTMENT, *November* 28, 1851.

SIR: Your letter of the 25th instant, in relation to further mail service for your steamers between New York and Liverpool, has been received.

You are informed, in reply, that this department concurs with the Postmaster General in his requirements of additional service by the mail steamers from New York to Liverpool, as expressed by him in his letter to this department, of which you have been furnished with a copy.

You will, therefore, be pleased to furnish a schedule of the days of sailing of the Liverpool mail steamers of your line at as early a day as practicable.

The subject relating to compensation will be referred by the Postmaster General for the consideration of Congress.

I am, very respectfully, your obedient servant,

WM. A. GRAHAM.

EDWARD K. COLLINS, Esq., and associates, New York.

The Postmaster General, in his annual report, also expressly refers to this subject, and recommends that an appropriation be made. I will read part of what he says:

"The contract with the Collins line of mail steamers between New York and Liverpool requires the performance of but twenty trips out and back during the year. For the purpose, however, of arranging *weekly* trips in American steamers, alternating with those of the Cunard steamers, which depart weekly from this country and England, these steamers have made departures each alternate week, and have thus completed a weekly line of American steamers from New York. If these trips are continued as heretofore, there will have been performed in the present year three more trips than are provided for in the contract, and to continue the weekly trips thereafter will require additional trips per year.

"As the English Government had made new arrangements, by which the weekly trips of the Cunard steamers were to be continued through the year, it was deemed highly important to continue the weekly trips of the American steamers also. Under these circumstances, Mr. Collins was requested to continue his trips every other week, and was assured that the payment by Congress of a *pro rata* compensation would be recommended. It is claimed by the contractors, and it is believed justly, that a *pro rata* compensation for these extra trips, in the winter season, will not fully indemnify them; and if the extra trips are performed, it is earnestly recommended that a *pro rata* compensation, with such addition, if any, as may be necessary to give the contractors a fair and liberal compensation for the extra service, be authorized by Congress. The unrivalled qualities and speed of the ships of this line, and the very satisfactory manner in which the service has been performed, establishing the superiority of American skill and enterprise in the construction of ocean steamers and in ocean steam navigation, entitle the proprietors of this line to the most favorable consideration, and I cannot doubt that Congress will make the appropriation recommended."

Here is the recommendation from the head of a department which is called for by Senators. There was also an estimate made by the department and submitted to the committee. This estimate was confined to the *pro rata* allowance mentioned by the Postmaster General. No estimate, of course, could be made by the department for such additional compensation as Congress might think proper to give for the purpose of sustaining this enterprise. I therefore submit that this amendment is not subject to the technical objection made by the Senator from Arkansas, (Mr. BORLAND.) We are not obliged to confine our action to the amount of the estimate. The whole subject is before us.

These additional trips were to be performed in the winter, with but few passengers, at an extraordinary expense; therefore a mere *pro rata* allowance would be no fair compensation.

Collins & Co. have submitted a statement showing the great losses which they have sustained in running their ships under the present contract; that statement has been verified by affidavit; and no Senator who is acquainted with the character and high honor of the persons conected with the Collins line would hardly require such a verification of their statements. At all events, the committee were entirely satisfied that these losses have been sustained; and I think I can satisfy the Senate that unless the company receives this additional compensation from the government the enterprise must fail.

I will now state to the Senate what will be the additional compensation proposed by the amendment. Under the original contract, they were to perform twenty trips a year, and receive for them $385,000, or $19,250 per trip. The six additional trips per year, under a *pro rata* allowance, would be $115,500—making for the year's service the sum of $500,500, under the present contract. The ammendment proposes to give them at the rate of $33,000 per trip for twenty-six trips, making $858,000 a year. This increases the compensation on the fifty-two trips $357,500, or $13,750 on each trip; but from this increase should be deducted the additional costs of running winter trips. In the statement of losses to which I have referred, there is given the cost of these ships, the actual average cost of every voyage, and the amount of capital invested. The cash cost of the steamers ready for sea is stated at $2,948,000—a little less than $300,000,000. The actual average cost of each voyage to England and back is stated at $65,215 64; the average receipts for each voyage at $48,286 85—making a deficiency of $16,928 70 on each voyage; which, for twenty trips, would amount to $338,575 80, and on twenty-six trips $440,148.

The Senate will perceive by this statement that the amount proposed by the amendment falls a few thousand dollars short of the loss which may be sustained upon the twenty-six trips to be run under the new arrangement.

I now wish to call the attention of the Senate to what I consider to have been the causes of these great losses sustained by the company. It has been asserted that they are owing to extravagance; that the ships are larger and more splended and costly than the company were bound to build by the contract. It is true that these ships are of a superior character in style, size, and power to those contemplated by the contract; but ought we to complain of that? The company may, in their laudable ambition to surpass their foreign rival, have expended more money than was required by their contract; but surely we ought not to take advantage of this, and object to their doing more for the success of this great enterprise than they were bound by law to do. But, sir, the most of these losses arose from other causes—from circumstances over which they had no control. One great cause of extra expenditure on the part of the company was owing to the fact that the enterprise was an entirely new one in this country—so new that when they commenced building their first ship it was found that the machinery and tools necessary for the construction of their powerful engines were not to be found in the country. These implements of construction had to be either procured from England, or made here at great expense; and large sums of money were necessarily expended in experiments upon this preliminary machinery required in the construction of the ships.

But that is not the principal cause of their losses. By the contract, Collins & Co. were not bound to build ships of the size and power of those they have constructed. They might have merely followed in the wake of the Cunard line, taken their ships as models, and imitate them in size and model, and been contented with their speed. But they felt, as every American citizen felt, that this was a great undertaking—that it was a national contest—and, in competing with Great Britain upon this subject of ocean mail steamers, they desired to produce to the country and to the world steamers a little superior to those built by Great Britain, and with which she then commanded the trade of the world. In accomplishing that they have made great sacrifices; but they have, by so doing, put afloat ships far superior to those of the Cunard line in power and speed. For this they have expended large sums of money, and sustained great losses upon their capital.

Another cause why they have lost money is, that the moment their ships were put afloat, they met with a active competion in England, backed by the influence of the English Government. It was not a mere struggle between Mr. Collins and Mr. Cunard. It was not a mere struggle between the enterprise of an American citizen and a subject of Queen Victoria, standing upon their individual capital, talent, and enterprise. No, sir; it was a contest with the English Government. The moment the Collins line was established, it became a national concern with the people and Government of England to put down the Collins line by extending encouragement to the Cunard line. At the same time, some of the first trips made by our steamers were unfortunate, and immediately the cry was raised in Europe, and especially in Great Britain, that they were not safe—consequently passengers refused to go in them and they made many trips in which they sustained great losses on account of this alarm.

It may be true, as stated by the Senator from Virginia, (Mr. Hunter,) that these gentlemen, under such circumstances, expended more money than they ought to have expended. But yet we all know the feeling which exists in the mind of every American for Brother Jonathan to beat John Bull in any enterprise of this character. Urged on by that national feeling, and, perhaps, carried to an extravagant extent, these gentlemen may have expended more money than was necessary to fulfil their contract; but surely they are not to be sacrificed on that account.

In accounting for the losses sustained by the Collins line, it is necessary also to compare the ships of his line with those of the Cunard line. By this comparison it will appear that this Government is enjoying the service of ships far superior in size, tonnage, power and speed to those of the Cunard line, and at a less compensation upon their relative costs and power of service. I have prepared a comparative statement of the two lines, which I here submit to the Senate:

COLLINS STEAMSHIPS.

Names.	Tonnage.	Horse power.	Capable of working.	Length.
1. Atlantic	3,000	1,000	1,500	274
2. Pacific	3,000	1,000	1,500	274
3. Baltic	3,000	1,000	1,500	280
4. Arctic	3,000	1,000	1,500	280
	12,000	4,000	6,000	

Baltic.............9 days.....13 hours...... 0 minutes from Liverpool to New York.
Arctic.............9 " ......13 " ......10 " from New York to Liverpool.

CUNARD STEAMSHIPS.

Names.	Tonnage.	Horse power.	Capable of working.	Length.
1. Africa	2,266	800	1,000	280
2. America	1,832	650	800	249
3. Asia	2,266	800	1,000	280
4. Cambia	1,423	500	700	217
5. Canada	1,832	650	800	249
6. Europa	1,832	650	800	249
7. Niagara	1,832	650	800	240
	13,282	4,700	5,900	

Asia......... { 10 days.....22 hours......30 minutes from Liverpool to New York.
{ 10 " ......12 " ......15 " from New York to Liverpool.

Asia	10 "	......22 "	......30 "	from Liverpool to New York.
Baltic	9 "	......13 "	...... 0 "	" "
Difference	1 "	...... 9 "	......30 "	of time.
Asia	10 "	......12 "	......15 "	from New York to Liverpool.
Arctic	9 "	......17 "	......10 "	" "
Difference	0 "	......19 "	...... 5 "	of time.

These are the principal reasons why this company have sustained the loss mentioned. But what has been their loss has been the country's gain. While they have been losing

$16,000 per trip, we have been gaining great national advantages. I will endeavor to show this. In the first place, great advantages have been accomplished for our commerce generally. In order to illustrate this, we must look back to the commencement of the navigation of the ocean by steamships.

England commenced this system in the year 1838. It is true that as far back as 1819 an American ship, called the "Savannah," had gone from New York to Liverpool, partly by sail and partly by steam, in twenty-six days. If the American Government at that time had taken up this new enterprise with the same energy and force with which the English Government afterwards took it up in 1838, we should have had the honor and the glory of being the first to establish successfully the navigation of the ocean by steamers. In 1838 the "Great Britain" was built. She sailed on the 8th of April of that year from Liverpool, with, in the language of the history of that time, "seven adventurous passengers;" and she arrived in New York after a passage of fifteen days. In 1839 the Cunard line was established by a contract made by the British Government with Mr. Cunard, of Halifax, in Nova Scotia, for carrying the mails twice a month from Liverpool via Halifax to Boston, for seven years, for £65,000, or $325,000. Afterwards the Government increased the compensation to £85,000, or $425,000—the service to be performed by ships of twelve hundred tons and four hundred and fifty horse power. Upon the establishment of the Collins line in 1849–'50, the English Government again increased the compensation of Mr. Cunard to £145,000, or 725,000, and not $697,000, as stated by the Senator from Virginia yesterday.

Mr. HUNTER. Does the Senator from New Jersey refer to the statement which I made as to what is given by the British Government to the Cunarders?

Mr. MILLER. I do.

Mr. HUNTER. Then I would say to the gentleman that that statement was obtained from the Senator from Texas, (Mr. RUSH,) the Chairman of the Committee on the Post Office and Post Roads, from a statement which was put into his hands by the Postmaster General. I received a letter from the Postmaster General requesting me to examine the statement, but somehow it was lost. But this memorandum was given to me by the Senator from Texas, and it is presumed to be the most authenticate account we have of what is given by the British Government to the Cunard steamships. The account was made out, I believe, by the admiralty itself.

Mr. MILLER. I know there are different statements in regard to what the English Government now pay to Mr. Cunard. I am informed—and I have confidence in the information—that the compensation is higher than I have stated, and that is now actually over $1,000,000 a year. But I have authority here for the amount which I have stated. It is Chambers's Papers for the People"—a work of great authority, published in Edinburg in 1851. It contains a chapter on the English ocean mail-routes, giving a full history of the rise, progress, and present state of the English policy upon this important subject. It is full of statistics, which must have been taken from the most authentic sources. I will read to the Senate what is stated to be the compensation received by Mr. Cunard in 1849, and the reason why it was then increased to the sum of £145,000:

"But with the exception of the voyage of the Savannah, in 1819, the citizens of the United States had not hitherto taken any part in conducting the steam navigation of the Atlantic; and it was not until after all but Cunard's ships had been withdrawn, that American built steamers began to ply between England aud New York. The formation of several companies for this purpose made Mr. Cuaard anxious to extend his contract, so as to carry the mails once a week, and thus render him more able to meet the expected competition. Mr. Cunard said before a committee of the House of Commons in July, 1849: 'I was most anxious to have it (the extention of the contract) done, because I knew the consequences of having these rival lines of packets running against us, and that it would affect the Government more than it would affect us. I could not increase the number of passengers; but the number of letters would be considerably increased, or doubled, bscause if one person writes, the whole must write.' The proposal was agreed to; the mails were to be carried from Liverpool every Saturday, and from Boston or New York every Wednesday, (except during four winter months, when it was to be fortnightly,) arrangements being made by which the detour to Halifax was to be abandoned. To effect this service the vessels must steam altogether about 272,800 miles every year, and for it Mr. Cunard was to receive £145,000 per annum. This is the contract now in force. Mr. Cunard considered not as a new arrangement, but as an extension of the old; and as the service was doubled, and as the postage revenue of the steamers had hitherto been equal to the contract money, he naturally supposed that the payment would now be doubled. But Mr. Goulburn, then Chancellor of the Exchequer, would not give more than £145,000, which Mr. Cunard said was 'a very unjust thing,' and quaintly added—'I beg to say this not with any disrespect to Mr. Goulburn: he did it to save the money to the country; but he took £25,000 a year from me for the good of the country.'"

This is the last contract that I have any certain information of, although I am informed that the compensation has been increased, in order to pay for the additional trips in winter. Mr. Cunard's "quaint" reply to the Chancellor of the Exchequer ought to be noticed. It might, with propriety, be used by Mr. Collins in answer to the Senator from Virginia, (Mr. Hunter.) Mr. Goulburn, the Chancellor of the Exchequer, acting in pretty much the same capacity in which my friend from Virginia acts, cut down the compensation to £145,000—on which Mr. Cunard said, "he did it to save the money of the country, but he took £25,000 a year from me for the good of the country." I have shown, therefore, upon what I considered good authority, that the Cunard line is now receiving $725,000 a year, instead of $696,000, or $15,000 a trip, instead of $13,000, as stated yesterday by my friend from Virginia.

Mr. BORLAND. I wish to understand fully the authority upon which the Senator from New Jersey relies in this case. I would ask him if all the information on this subject, as far as it relates to the action of the British Government, is not to be found in the official records of the proceedings of that Government, and whether they are not to be had in this city? I understand that we interchange official records with the British Government, and I apprehend that all their official action in regard to this matter is to be found in these records, which must necessarily be more reliable than a popular publication, made, I do not know whether in this country or in England, and thrown into general circulation—a sort of newspaper publication. I think, in a matter of this importance, involving facts which lie at the bottom of this question, we shall have as authority, official information, which I apprehend our Post Office Department has, and which is probably in the Library of Congress, or in some of the departments of the Government. I would prefer, for that reason, to rely on official authority rather than on this popular publication.

Mr. HUNTER. The statement of $696,000 a year, which I derived from the chairman of the Committee on the Post Office and Post Roads, I used because I supposed he had the most authentic information. He derived it from that document, to which my attention was directed by the Postmaster General. I confess that I had supposed before that the amount given the Cunard line was about £140,000 sterling per annum. It would not, however, vary it much if you were to take that amount; for the difference between $725,000 and $696,000 is not very great.

Mr. MILLER. I will answer the question of the honorable Senator from Arkansas. I have no knowledge at all of their being any official information in the departments here such as he speaks of. I think there is none. The author I have quoted may be relied upon; his statements appear to be taken from the official documents in Great Britain, and if the gentleman will take the trouble of reading the article I think he will be satisfied of its authenticity.

Mr. BORLAND. The Senator misunderstood me if he supposed I questioned at all the authority. I simply called attention to the character of the work. I said that I would prefer, in the formation of my opinions, to have official information. The Senator says I would find that it contained a good deal of authentic information. I might find a great deal of information in it, but surely, taking it as one of what we might call the "fugitive publications" of the day, I should not know, unless it was from an official source, whether the information was authentic or not. That is the point.

Mr. MILLER. The Senator asked me a question and I have answered it. The regulation of the Cunard steamers, I understand, is under the control of the admiralty, and are connected somewhat with the war service; these compensations are increased or diminished without having a special law passed by Parliament for the purpose. I also understand that since the Cunard line was ordered up to additional weekly service, during the last year the compensation has been again increased. But as I have no information upon this point other than that which has been stated to me by gentlemen here, I do not rely upon it as a fact in my argument.

The keel of the first steamer on the Collins line was laid in 1849, and their first steamer left New York about the beginning of the year 1850. What was the condition of things at that time? I call the attention of the Senate to it for the purpose of showing what has been accomplished since by this line. At that time Great Britain had the monopoly of all the foreign postage to this country. She had also driven off our sailing packets from the carrying of passengers. She had beaten them off in the transportation of all light articles of merchandise, and of specie, and of all transportations across the Atlantic which depend upon time, speed, and certainty. Up to 1840, the American sailing packets had the control of these matters. They had beaten the English packets away from even a competition in the carrying of passengers, specie, and light merchandise. England then resorted to ocean steam navigation. Her Government, finding that her sailing vessels were beaten by the Yankee vessels, resorted to steam, and by a most liberal policy she built up the Cunard line; and such had been the success of this policy that on the day when the keel of the first steamer of the Collins line was laid, England had a complete mastery of the ocean on all these great interests. What has taken place since? It must be recollected that, in the carrying of letters and passengers, speed and certainty are everything. By the establishment of the Collins line we have beaten them upon both of these points. By our line we carry letters and passengers in less time than the Cunard line can carry them. By the accounts of the very last arrival of the steamers, we are informed that, although one of the Cunard line left Liverpool four days before the Collins line, yet the mails of the two steamers were delivered simultaneously at the post office here. This is what the Collins has accomplished in this great race of national steamers.

The carrying of light articles of freight and of specie has become a very important matter in our foreign commerce. Before the establishment of the Collins line, it was altogether under the control of the Cunard line. We may now control it ourselves if we will but sustain our own people. We beat England with our sailing-vessels, and we will beat her with our steamships, if this Government will only protect our commerce with the same liberality with which the English Government has protected hers. That is the great question in this case.

The English Government and the English people are very wise, and very liberal, too, with regard to the management of their own great interests. They do not accomplish as many magnificent projects as we do; but they have a keener eye to their own interests. We established a line of mail steam-packets to Havre and Bremen. They bring freight and passengers from the continent, by way of Havre and Bremen, to New York. Now, what do we find the Cunard line doing? Why, in order to cripple our line, and secure to themselves the monopoly of the carrying trade from the continent, the proprietors of the Cunard line have, I understand, established a line of small steamers, running from Liverpool to Havre, by which they carry, free of charge, all goods from that point to Liverpool intended to be conveyed in their steamers to the United States. This they have done, and are now doing. The very last packet which arrived brought this piece of foreign news.

"Belgium.—The Belgium papers state that it is the intention of the Cunard line to establish a line of steamers between Antwerp and Liverpool, to connect with the American line."

Is it not evident that England is endeavoring to control the passengers, the freight, and the postage from the continent to the United States?—and that, unless we sustain our line of steamers, she will control all these great interests?

I desire here to call the attention of the Senate to the effect produced upon the public mind of England by the establishment of the Collins line. I read from the same authority, (Chambers:)

"The American steamers that first plied regularly on the American route were the Washington and Hermann, of about two thousand tons burden. They, however, did not depend entirely on the British traffic, but made the port of Bremen, at the mouth of the river Weser, in Germany, their terminus in Europe, calling at Southampton on their passage up and down the British Channel. The line of vessels that enter into direct competition with Cunard's, was projected by Mr. Collins, of New York, and consisted of five steamers of three thousand tons burden, three hundred feet long, and propelled by engines of one thousand horse power. They are named after the various oceans of the world—the Atlantic, Pacific, Arctic, Baltic, and Adriatic. They are longer and more powerful than any steamer yet built, except the Great Britain, and their competition is not to be treated lightly. The merits of the rival lines will become a national question.

"Thus was commenced that rivalry which has made a gigantic race-course of the Atlantic ocean—a race-course so long that the difference in the longitude of its termini makes a difference of nearly five hours in the time of day; and thus, while the people at the American end are rising from their beds, those at the European have got through much of their day's work. The 'flying horse Childers,' and other notables of the turf, have done great deeds in their way, but they shrink into utter insignificance compared with the performances of a steamer propelled by a steamer equal to that of a thousand horses, sailing three hundred miles each day, over angry, restless waves, twenty-four, and sometimes forty-three feet high, chasing each other at a distance of about five hundred feet, and at a speed of more than thirty miles an hour. All the prizes of the turf are paltry compared with that for which these steamers are contending—the proud distinction of establishing the most speedy and safe communication between two great continents, and two mighty nations. Hitherto the superiority has not been distinctly declared on either side, nor can any correct judgment be formed until at least a year has elapsed."

But what is more important in this case is, to show what has been the result of the establishment of the Collins line upon our interests at home. In the first place, its effect upon our treasury, of which we have heard much: Have we lost money by it? By the statement furnished by the Post Office Department, and laid before the Senate by the Senator from California, it appears that we have not lost a cent, but, on the contrary, gained $58,675 59. That statement shows that the revenue derived by the United States under the operation of the treaty and by the establishment of

the Collins line is - - - - -	$828,675 59
Of which there had been paid to Collins, for his service for two years - - - -	770,000 00
	$58,675 59

Or nearly $30,000 per annum into the hands of the Government, over and above what they have paid. I do not pretend that all this postage was derived from letters or newspapers carried by the Collins line. No man can understand the account in that way. But it is nevertheless true that all this postage, whether received from Cunard's line or Collins's line, has been received in consequence of that policy which established the Collins line. There was no postal treaty made between this Government and Great Britain, until the keel of the first steamer of the Collins line was laid; and we should have had no control whatever of this postage fund had not the Collins line been established and put in competition with the Cunard line. So far, then, as the policy is concerned, and its effect upon the treasury, the Collins line is entitled to the credit for the mony received for postage, against the charge for the money which has been paid for its support.

It is true that the amount received during the last year will not cover the amount proposed to be given by this amendment; yet this does not prove that the receipts of the coming year will not be sufficient to cover the appropriation. There is already an increase of postage this year. The increase in the number of trips by both lines will add to the amount. That has been the result heretofore. As the number of trips and speed of the steamers have been increased, the postage receipts have advanced, and therefore, in considering this proposition, we can safely rely that for the coming year there will be a considerable increase of the postal revenue. Heretofore the Collins line performed only monthly trips during the winter, and the Cunard semi-monthly. Now, they alternate weekly during the whole year; and although there are not as many passengers in these winter trips, there are just as many, and perhaps more, letters in the winter season. I shall not go into the estimate of this obvious increase of postage; but it is manifest that by this great increase of service there will be a corresponding increase in the postages received during the next year. The Postmaster General states that the increase of trans-Atlantic postages in 1851 over 1850 is $197,439 61. It will be much greater in 1852; so that my friend from Virginia need not be afraid of the treasury being ruined by this appropriation. It must also be recollected that unless we increase the service of our line, we will not be able to divide the postage with our competitors. England gets much the largest proportion of the postage now; but the moment we put our service upon an equality with hers, we shall be entitled to divide the whole postage, and put half of it into our treasury.

But the advantage to be derived from maintaining this line is not to be confined to a mere calculation of the amount of postage that may be put into the treasury. There are other considerations of much higher importance. The great route now from England, and from western Europe, to the East Indies, is from Southampton, by way of Gibraltar and Alexandria. But who does not perceive that the time is coming, that it is not far distant, when the great mail-route to the East Indies, not only from New York, but from London and from Paris, will be over the Atlantic, and by either of the Cunard line or of the Collins line, under the control either of the English Government or of the American Government. That presents this important question to the Senate and to the country, whether we shall not at all hazards sustain this line, in order to preserve for our people, and for our Government, the control of that great world's route which is to pass along the shores of this country, and across the Isthmus of Panama, and thence to the East Indies?

The honorable Senator from Virginia said that if this line could not sustain itself, let it go down. The Cunard line will not go down. The great West India mail steam-route of England will not go down. But if our lines alone goes down, what happens? All the communication—the passengers, the letters, and the commerce, passing over the Atlantic, crossing the Isthmus of Panama to the Pacific ocean, and there spreading out to the great East—will be under the complete control of the English Government. But if you sustain the American line of steamers—and if this route turns out, as I believe it will, to be the most direct route, from London, and from Western Europe, to China—our line, having the superiority in speed, and of certainty, will be the grand carrier of letters and of passengers from Europe, through America, to the East Indies.

It is stated in the book from which I have already quoted that last year a letter written in the city of New York, passing in the Cunard line to England, and then put on board the steamer at Southampton, thence by way of Alexandria to Suez, reached Hong Kong in fifty-five days.

Now, sir, it is reduced to almost a certainty, that a letter written in London, passing with the speed of the Collins line over the Atlantic, and by Panama to the Pacific, will reach the same place in forty days. This route is ours! The great commerce of the world by steam is thus under our control.

Yet, the honorable Senator says: Let this line go down; or let it fight its way as best it can under the protection of individual enterprise.

As I said before, our people can contend single-handed with any people on the face of the earth; but they cannot contend with the capitalists of Great Britain, backed by the protection of the English Government. They may contend with them for a short time, but the stubborn endurance of John Bull will break down the enterprise even of a Yankee, unless he be also supported by his own Government. Therefore, I say, throwing aside the matter of dollars and cents—whether it costs us a few thousand dollars, more or less—here are national considerations which should induce us to sustain this line. There are also other considerations. By the contract these ships are to be made war steamers; and I intend to show they are war steamers—the best of the kind in the world for certain purposes of war, and that they can, at small expense, be used as such in any emergency. I have here a letter of Commodore Perry on this subject, dated February 18, 1852, and addressed to the Secretary of the Navy. Speaking of these ships—the Collins line—he says:

"According to my calculations, the cost of the conversion of either the before-mentioned vessels, exclusive of armaments, repair of machinery, &c., would not, or certainly ought not to cost for each steamer over $20,000; and it could readily be done for this at any of our navy-yards. With respect to the description and weight of their respective armaments, I am clearly of the opinion that the first class steamers already named could easily carry four 10-inch Paixhan guns on pivots—two forward and two aft—of the weight of those in the Mississippi, and ten 8-inch Paixhan guns on the sides; and this armament would not incommode the vessels, and the weight less than the ice, which is usually forty tons, and stowed away in one mass."

Commodore Perry continues, that—

"In the general operations of a maritime war, they could render good service, and especially would they be useful from their great speed as despatch vessels, and for the transportation of troops, always capable of attack and defence, and of overhauling or escaping from an enemy.

"The Atlantic, Pacific, Baltic, and Arctic have all been built, inspected, and received by the Navy Department."

Commodore Perry adds to this letter a *note*, and says, "that an ocean steamer of 3,000 tons is of the maximum dimension for safety and efficiency, whether for *war* or commercial purposes."

At the time of the construction of these ships every attention was given to their form, strength, and models by the contractors, under the special direction of the Navy Department. To show that, I will merely refer to the communications upon the subject. They are as follows:

E. K. Collins's letter to the Secretary of the Navy, in relation to the *side-lever engine*, with the Secretary of the Navy's approval.

E. K. Collins's letter to the Secretary of the Navy, asking for consent to modify specifications, with the answer of the

Secretary of the Navy that Commodore Skinner, of the Bureau of Construction, had approved of the alteration.

E. K. Collins's letter to the Secretary of the Navy, asking for the appointment of a naval constructor and superintendent, with Secretary of the Navy's answer, appointing Capt. S. Skiddy naval constructor.

Secretary of the Navy's answer to E. K. Collins, accepting the Arctic, with report of Commodore Perry and Commander Bell to Secretary of the Navy, in reference to the capacity and usefulness of the Arctic for war purposes.

United States Navy-Yard,
Philadelphia, April 14, 1852.

Sir: In answer to yours of the 13th, I have to state, as chief naval constructor, the specifications for building the Collins line of steamers were submitted to me, and approved, as in accordance with the act of 3d of March, 1847.

They can be converted into war steamers to carry a battery equal to our largest steam-frigates, in a short time, and the necessary alterations to be made to receive such a battery will not exceed a cost of $20,000 each.

I am, sir, with great respect, your obedient servant,
FRANCIS GRICE.

To the Hon. Wm. M. Gwin,
United States Senate, Washington.

It appears by these letters, which are on file in the Navy Department, that the vessels have been constructed with special reference for war service; that naval officers of high character and great experience were not only consulted in their construction, but superintended their building, who all say that they are capable of being used in case of war, at the small expense of about $20,000 each.

I submit to the Senate whether this is not a consideration which should induce us to sustain these ships, and to keep them under the control of the Government, to be used in the case of war? No man who has seen these ships—no man who has heard these evidences—can doubt for a moment but that they would be, at this very hour, if war should break out, the most effective steamships now under our control. They may not be as strong as war steamers especially constructed for the purpose. They may not be as powerful as many ships constructed by the English Government; but their great utility would be their speed and their power of action. If we can, by an expenditure of $20,000, put these splendid ships into the war service, that of itself is a sufficient consideration for us to appropriate this money, in order to keep them afloat. We cannot maintain or keep up war steamers of equal power at anything like as cheap a rate as we can these steamers.

With regard to the capacity of these ships, and their usefulness in war, my honorable colleague, who has had great experience upon this subject, will, I have no doubt, sustain me in the opinion I have expressed, that these ships will be of great service to the country in time of war. These steamers surpass in speed any vessel which has yet been constructed by the Government, with all the advantages and experience of the navy in the construction of ships.

I noticed that the United States steamship San Jacinto arrived at Cadiz on the 25th of March, having left Norfolk on the third of the month. Twenty-two days steaming only thirty-five hundred miles, or one hundred and fifty-nine miles per day.

Mr. STOCKTON. That ship was built on an entirely different plan.

Mr. MILLER. I intend to compare her speed with the Collins line, and to state that, at this rate of steaming, it it would require nineteen days for the passage from New to Liverpool, instead of nine and a half days. My colleague states, however, that that ship was built upon entirely different principle, and therefore there cannot be any fair comparison betwen them.

I have called the attention of the Senate to the speed, the models, and the capacity of these vessels for another purpose, that is to show that this company have, in executing this enterprise, made experiments, secured information, and given models of steamships, with their engines, of great practical value to the public. If we never received a cent of pcstage we should be fully compensated for the money we have paid by the increased knowledge we have received with regard to the building of ocean steamers. Collins & Co. have, at an immense expense of time and money, rendered all these services to the country, and we have reaped all the advantage of their enterprise. They have sustained all the loss. I say, therefore, that these considerations ought to enter into the minds of Senators when they vote on this proposition.

Again: the building and running of these ships have produced to the country a class of practical engineers that it would not have had without this undertaking. It has been a school for our young engineers. These vessels are now every year training up engineers, who are to take charge of our steam ships of war, or to be employed in the commercial marine. Thus the country is acquiring knowledge at the expense of the owners of the Collins line. This, also, ought to be taken into consideration. So great has been the cost, and so perfect the skill in the construction of these ships and of their machinery, that no accident of any moment has happened to them.

Mr. HALE. The Atlantic broke her shaft.

Mr. MILLER. True; but it was one which was made in England!

In advocating the policy of our Government sustaining these steamers, I wish to call the attention of the Senate and the country to what Great Britain is doing upon this subject of ocean mail-steamers, not only with regard to the Cunard line, but in regard to many other lines. She has established five great routes of ocean mail-steamers. I do not speak now of her inland steam postal arrangements. She has now under contract with the admiralty sixty-three ocean mail steamers, every one of which may be converted into war steamers. The aggregate power of these steamers is twenty-nine thousand six hundred and twenty horse power; their tonnage is sixty-one thousand three and forty-eight; they annually steam one million five hundred and seventy-five thousand miles; and the aggregate amount paid by the Government for mail service performed on these several routes is about $4,000,000. These routes are, first, the Atlantic route from Liverpool to New York; the second is the route to the West Indies and the eastern coast of South America. That route has its depot at St. Thomas, from which point eight branch routes, employing about twenty steamers, are extended to the adjacent islands to the principal cities in Central and South America, and on the Gulf of Mexico. The third route is the great East India line, which sails twice a month from Southampton, in England, touching at Gibraltar, and then to Alexandria, thence by overland route for a short distance, take steam again at Suez to Calcutta, and Bombay, and China. The fourth is the route by way of the Cape of Good Hope. The fifth is the Pacific route from Valparaiso to Panama. There are several other proposed routes, which I understand have been contracted for, to Australia and other portions of the East. I have prepared tabular statements of these different routes, showing the number of steamers, tonnage, power, and the miles steamed.

From Southampton to West Indies and South America.

Names of Steamers.	Length.	Horse power.	Tonnage.
Avon	216	430	1,881
Clyde	213	430	1,841
Conway	186	300	929
Dee	214	410	1,848
Eagle	164	250	501
Great Western	207	400	1,467
Medway	212	420	1,666
Reindeer	155	260	554
Serein	215	430	1,886
Tay	214	430	1,858
Tevoit	214	430	1,793
Thames	215	420	1.676
Trent	215	420	1,666

The number of miles steamed annually is six hundred and eighty-four thousand eight hundred and sixteen, (684,816) or not less than thirty times the circumference of the globe.

The steamships of this company traverse routes twenty-seven degrees north of the tropic of Cancer to twelve degrees south of the tropic of Capricorn—embracing in their circuit every island of importance in the West Indies, or the west coast of Africa, seaports around the gulf of Mexico, the great cities of South America, and bestow the blessings of a postal communication for every civilized nation.

	Horse power.	Tonnage.	Miles annually steamed.
Pacific Company from Panama to Valparaiso. This company possesses five steamers, average tonnage.......	995	3,000	110,887
Cape of Good Hope Company—just commenced monthly in vessels not less than (each)........................	200	....	80,400

ROUTE TO THE EAST INDIES.

1st. From Falmouth to Gibraltar.
2d. From Gibraltar to Alexandria.
3d. From Suez to Bombay.
4th. From Bombay to Calcutta.
5th. From Calcutta to Madras, Ceylon, and China.

All of these routes are now formed under one company, called the *"Peninsular and Oriental Company."*

MEDITERRANEAN AND PENINSULAR SERVICE.

Names of Steamships.	Length.	Horse power.	Tonnage.
Erin	199	280	797
Euxine	222	400	1,165
Ganges	237	500	1,200
Iberia	155	190	515
Jupiter	158	210	543
Madrid	163	140	478
Montrose	166	242	606
Pasha	160	210	548
Singapore	237	500	1,200
Sultan	224	420	1,090
Tagus	182	286	782

Between Southampton and Alexandria.

Names of Steamships.	Length.	Horse power.	Tonnage.
Hindostan	217	620	2,017
Indus	208	450	1,782
Ripon	231	450	1,925

Between Suez and Calcutta, via Ceylon and Madras.

Names of Steamships.	Length.	Horse power.	Tonnage.
Bentick	217	520	1,974
Haddington	217	450	1,647
Oriental	220	420	1,787
Precurser	229	460	1,817

Between Ceylon and Hong Kong, via Singapore.

Names of Steamships.	Length.	Horse power.	Tonnage.
Achilles	205	420	992
Braganza	188	264	855
Lady Mary Wood	160	260	553
Malta	205	460	1,217
Pekin	214	400	1,182
Pottinger	220	450	1,350

Between Hong Kong and Canton.

Canton	172	150	348

All these vessels with their contract with the admiralty, "are to be good, substantial (and efficient) steam-vessels, of such construction and strength as to be fit and able to carry guns of the largest calibre now used on board of her Majesty's steam-vessels-of-war."

Number of miles steamed annually by this company, three hundred and eighty-one thousand nine hundred and sixty, (381,960.)

PROPOSED ROUTES BY GREAT BRITAIN.

1st. From Panama (?) across the Pacific to the Gallapalos islands, thence to Sydney.

2d. From Cape of Good Hope, across the Indian ocean, to Western Australia.

3d. From Singapore, via East India islands, to Eastern Australia.

Recapitulation.—Number of steamships, 63; horse power, 29,620; tonnage, 61,348; miles steamed, 1,571,063.

I will also read to the Senate a description of this great Oriental route. Its extent and magnitude are astonishing:

"At Suez, at the head of the Red sea, two steamers are in waiting for the passengers and mails conveyed from Alexandria in small steamers up the Nile, and in vans across the desert. One of the steamers at Suez belongs to the East India Company, and has Bombay for its destination; the other is the property of the Oriental Company. The tenth of the month is fixed as the day of departure: and all persons and things having been shipped, the vessels steamed down the Red sea to Adeu, distant from Suez 1,308 miles. Here they part company; the Oriental steamer pursues a course almost due east, across the Indian ocean, to Point de Galle, in the Island of Ceylon—a distance of 2,134 miles. Having exchanged mails with the vessel for China, she steams up the Coromandel coast to Madras, and on to Calcutta, where she arrives in about twenty-eight days from Suez, after traversing 4,757 miles, and spending in stoppages about five days.

"The vessel in waiting at Point de Galle, as soon as she receives what the other has brought her, starts eastward, and after traversing 1,286 miles, arrives at Penang, in the peninsular of Malacca; from thence, steaming down between Sumatra and the main land, she arrives at the little island of Singapore, almost nnder the line, and then up the Chinese sea, terrible for its typhoons, to Hong Kong, where the little steamer in No 5 is ready to continue the line of communication to Canton.

"The Indian mail which left Southampton in August last, filled 157 chests, each capable of holding 10,000 letters, and at Malta 120 smaller chests were added that had been brought through France. Making allowance for the newspapers contained in these, the number of letters must still have been enormous. All this writing and transmission of intelligence necessarily increases trade, and consequently bring additional supplies of articles to this country, the duties on which must more than make up the difference between the payments to the companies and the revenues of the post office. But on the higher considerations than those of mere profit and loss, we have no hesitation in saying that the blessings to the country of these lines of speedy communication would not be purchased dearly if not one farthing of the contract money were returned."

"The number of miles steamed by the vessels of this company, under contract, is 381,960, and the payment $204,500 per annum. The company makes an annual dividend of eight per cent. on the capital of about £1,000,000; and supposing that the same fleet was kept up, and the revenue reduced to that derived from passengers and merchandise alone, not only could no dividend be paid, but an actual loss sustained every year of more than £120,000—another striking illustration of a fact already adverted to, that, without a post office contract such schemes of regular and efficient ocean steam navigation could not be maintained."

This shows that, although the proprietors of this Oriental line now divide eight per cent. dividend per annum, if the contract under which they carry the mails were taken away, it could not be sustained, but that there would be a loss of £126,000 per annum.

There is no doubt about what is the policy of England. She looks to the great return to her commerce and to her manufactures; and if not a cent of money is added to her revenue, by means of her postal contracts, yet she would be the gainer by establishing and keeping up these immense lines of steam navigation. These sixty-three ocean steamers, with a tonnage of 61,348, steaming 1,571,000 miles per annum, are under the control of the admiralty, and are capable of being converted, at any time, into war steamers. Now, Senators, look at the policy of England! By her lines of steamers she has surrounded the world. We all remember that striking simile of England's military power, "that the roll of her drum is heard from the rising to the setting of the sun." That figure will be changed. War and conquest will give way to peace and commerce, and the ring of the ocean steamer's bell will be heard on every sea, and along every coast, bell pealing to bell, the world round.

With these facts before us—with this mighty demonstration made and making by the English Government for the commerce of the world—are we to stand still and to doubt about keeping up the most important line of war steamers that we have afloat? No, sir. While gentlemen alarm themselves about him they call the Bear of Russia, and are terrified lest he may march an army across Asia—"dragging its slow length along," with all its cumbersome and costly appendages, and thereby control the destinies of the world!—yes, sir, while we are dreaming over transcendental ideas about the trodden-down nations of Europe—England is ploughing the oceans from pole to pole with her mighty fleet of steamers, and sowing the *seeds of commerce* and of trade from which she will hereafter reap a harvest such as no nation on this earth ever garnered before. That is her policy—it should be ours. It is our mission. It is the mission of commerce to civilize the world. It is commerce, aided by steam, that is to carry those principles of liberty and enterprise which have given to this country its prominence and its glory throughout the world to the other races and nations of mankind. I am for sustaining this policy. I am for keeping up these lines. I am for increasing them. And as soon as a communication is opened between the Atlantic and the Pacific—as soon as the dream of the old Spaniard shall be fully realized—I am for continuing this great route of steam commercial navigation across the Pacific, and in order to meet England with her great line which passes from Southampton to Alexandria, the Indian seas to China. Then the two great nations of the world—of one blood, decending from the same great stock—will, by means of the enterprise of their citizens, protected and defended by their respective Governments, carry commerce and civilization round the world. An honorable Senator suggests that we will have to fight for it. That may be, but I think the fight is going on now. That fight is between Collins and Cunard. The English Government stands by her man. He failed once, and broke down; but the Government put him on his feet again. Collins says he is now in the same postion; that he wants a little of the sinews of war—$14,000 more per trip—in order to sustain the contest. The question is whether this Government will do for him what the English Government did for Cunard—sustain our man in this fight? I much prefer this war of steam and commerce to any other war. No blood will be spilt in it. The "sinews of war" employed are only a little money; and if the Government will only stand by its citizens in the contest, the victory is won.

But the honorable Senator from Virginia says that this would be encouraging a monopoly. My object is directly the contrary. We established this line for the purpose of putting down monopoly which England had over our commerce. Let me say to the honorable Senator that, if the Collins line goes down or is withdrawn, then there will be a monopoly over which we shall have no control. The English Government will have the control of the transportation of every letter and every pound of specie, of passengers, and of most of the freights from and to Europe. Then, indeed, we shall be subject to a complete monopoly.

Again: it is said that if we protect this branch of business, we should protect other branches. Sir, I am willing to sustain every branch of American labor and American enterprise which needs protection against English capital and English combination. Whenever we find England, by means of Government patronage, building up and protecting her manufactures, we should give the like protection to the same kind of manufactures in this country, unless we intend to yield entirely to her. The gentleman referred to the iron manufactures of the country. I know that they need protection. Every man who has examined their prostrate condition must admit that they require protection at once by some modification of the present tariff laws. While I give my vote for the purpose of protecting American enterprise and labor employed in commerce, I am also ready and anxious to give proper protection to the manufacturers of iron and other manufactures in the country. I go for the principle, and will stand by one and all of the great American interests to sustain them against this overbearing competition of England.

Again: it is said that if we grant the favor to New York, other cities will be coming in and asking similar favors. Now, in the first place, I do not consider this is a favor granted to the city of New York. I look upon it as a national question, in which we are all concerned. I look upon it as a matter of policy for the whole country, and that every city in the

Union is as much interested in this policy as New York itself. But if the gentleman will bring forward for any city a case like this, where there is competition between an American and an English line of steamers, I will go for sustaining the American line. For instance, we have now established, or are about to establish, a line from New Orleans to Mexico. If England establishes a line along side of it, I am ready to protect our line against any competition that England may bring against it.

But I know of no such case. It is easy to defeat an application of this kind, by saying that if you grant this you may grant others. Wait till they come, and let us judge of every case upon its own merits. It turns out, upon examination of the petitions sent here, that twenty-one cities of this Union have petitioned in favor of this appropriation; and I have not heard of more than one remonstrance against it; and that is from the city of New York. I have not heard the slightest objection to this allowance from any other city of the Union. I have no doubt that there is some opposition to it in the city of New York; but that opposition is confined to a very few.

I have thus presented my views with regard to this subject. I have done so at much length, for I consider it to be one of high importance to the country. I must beg pardon of the Senate for having trespassed so long upon its attention.

SPEECH

OF

HON. C. T. JAMES,

OF RHODE ISLAND,

ON

THE COLLINS LINE OF STEAMERS.

DELIVERED

IN THE SENATE OF THE UNITED STATES,

MAY 6, 1852.

"As an American citizen, I thank Heaven that my country has never succumbed to a foreign power. Her flag still waves in all its glory, and is respected by every civilized nation on earth. Nor would I strike our flag of commerce. It has achieved a most important though peaceful victory, and I will not give my vote to have it furled, or struck to any foreign rival."

WASHINGTON:
PRINTED BY JOHN T. TOWERS.
1852.

SPEECH

OF

HON. C. T. JAMES,

OF RHODE ISLAND,

ON

THE COLLINS LINE OF STEAMERS.

DELIVERED

IN THE SENATE OF THE UNITED STATES,

MAY 6, 1852.

"As an American citizen, I thank Heaven that my country has never succumbed to a foreign power. Her flag still waves in all its glory, and is respected by every civilized nation on earth. Nor would I strike our flag of commerce. It has achieved a most important though peaceful victory, and I will not give my vote to have it furled, or struck to any foreign rival."

WASHINGTON:
PRINTED BY JNO. T. TOWERS.
1852.

SPEECH.

The Senate having under consideration the bill to supply deficiencies in the appropriations for the service of the fiscal year ending June 30, 1852, the pending question being on the amendment proposed by the Committee on Finance, as follows:

"For additional compensation for increasing the transportation of the United States mail between New York and Liverpool, in the Collins line of steamers, to twenty-six trips per annum, at such times as shall be directed by the Postmaster General, and in conformity to his last annual report to Congress, and his letter of the fifteenth of November last to the Secretary of the Navy, commencing said increased service on the first of January, eighteen hundred and fifty-two, at the rate of thirty three thousand dollars per trip, in lieu of the present allowance, the sum of two hundred and thirty-six thousand five hundred dollars."

Mr. JAMES said: Mr. PRESIDENT, I am fully aware that the Senate has become tired of the discussion of this amendment; and I am tired of it myself, as I believe the people are tired of hearing of it. Nothing would induce me, sir, to lengthen out the debate by taking part in it, but a sense of duty to my constituents, to the people of this country, and to myself as an American citizen. I deem the question one of great importance, not only to individual interests, but, in a national point of view, to the whole American people. It is simply for this reason that I feel a deep interest in the question. Novice as I am, sir, in parliamentary affairs, I cannot expect to cope with honorable Senators of far greater powers and much longer experience, nor yet to add much weight to the arguments already advanced in support of this measure; much less can I hope to bring home conviction to the mind of the honorable Senator from Virginia, to whom I regret to find myself opposed. I hope, however, that powerful and discerning mind will yet discover the error of its ways as regards this important subject; and when that shall occur, I know the honorable Senator's high sense of honor will not withhold an acknowledgment.

Mr. President, I do not propose to take up the time of the Senate by attempting a thorough investigation of the subject now before us, with a view to ascertaining the precise number of dollars and cents which this Government should advance to enable the Collins line of ocean steamers to compete successfully with their old, skilled, and experienced antagonists of the British Cunard line. I would, however, take a brief, practical, general view of the subject; and however imperfect that view may be, I trust it may be found truthful, if not satisfactory and convincing. I trust, also, that whatever I may say will be national in its character and bearing.

The honorable Senator from Virginia, (Mr. HUNTER,) whom I am always pleased to hear on this floor, because, however I may differ from his views on this question, always brings great force and power to his aid on any subject that calls him out, assumed the other day that the amount to be paid by the Government in aid of this enterprise would be so much paid for protection against foreign competition. The honorable gentleman then added, and very properly, too, in my opinion, that there were other interests equally meritorious which stand in as much need of protection as the Collins line of steamers—such as manufactures of iron, woollen, and other articles. I have the pleasure to agree most fully with the honorable gentleman on this point, and can but hope that we may not disagree on a partial remedy for the evils experienced in all these cases.

But, Mr. President, the honorable Senator stated, I think, that to extend pecuniary aid to the Collins line of steamers would be protection in its worst form. Whether worst or best, however, sir, it is the only available form. For the Government to discriminate between this line and the British line, by means of custom duties, port charges, &c., would be a direct infraction of treaty stipulations; and hence the only protection we can extend to the American line is pecuniary aid from the national treasury. But as the honorable Senator from Virginia incidentally introduced the subject of protection to manufacturers, it may not be deemed irrelevant should I, in passing, stop to offer a remark or two on that subject as incidental to the question now before us.

It is an idea that has long been considered by many as an incontrovertible fact that any aid bestowed by Government on any branch of business, in the form of discriminating duties, or otherwise, is a tax imposed on the consumer, and to be paid by him, in addition to what would otherwise be the cost of the article consumed, and that for the sole benefit of the manufacturer or producer. In other words, that, if the purchaser were to pay a duty of 20 per cent. *ad valorem* on the article purchased, the domestic and foreign fabriç both would be enhanced 20 per cent. in price to the consumer, which addition would become a perpetual tax, and find its way into the pocket of the manufacturer or producer to enhance his profits.

No doubt, Mr. President, this idea has been, and is, very honestly entertained and advocated; yet I think it is a mistake, and feel well assured that there are facts in abundance to prove it so. But I am not about to go into the argument on this subject at the present time, and will merely notice one or two facts to illustrate what I have said.

It is believed, sir, that all articles of manufacture produced in the United States, iron included, the manufacture of which may be said to have gained a firm footing, and been fostered so as to enable them to compete with similar foreign articles, have continually diminished in price to the present moment, and are to be had at less prices in our own market than in any other market in the world. In fact, the reduction of price in most articles has been more than double the amount of protective duties that have been imposed on similar articles from foreign countries. Certainly this does not look very much like taxing the consumer.

It is truly essential to success, and therefore as important to all branches of business, especially manufactures, that skill and practical knowledge should be obtained by long and close application and thorough training in regular practical operations, and as much so as that candidates for office in our army and navy should be trained in our military or naval schools, and in the field or on shipboard be made practically acquainted with the duties of their professions. The evidence of the benefits of such a course of training with the artisan and the operative is to be seen in every city, town, village and hamlet, and on the person of every citizen, in the astonishing improvements that have been made in every department of the mechanic arts, and the equally astonishing reduction that has been effected in the cost of almost every production.

Mr. President, in the very nature of things it is impossible for our mechanics and operatives to compete with those of

Europe in those branches in which their mechanical ingenuity has not been called out and developed. Practice is necessary. We have as good mechanical ability as any country on the globe, and practice, and practice alone, is necessary to its full development. When government grants to that ability protection against foreign competition, it calls it into successful action, and whether in the manufacture of cloth or iron, or the construction and management of steamships, or any thing else, that talent will not fail to return to the government and the country a thousand fold for all the protection thus granted.

Permit me, sir, to ask, how is our mechanical talent to be fully developed? How are our artisans, our engineers, and our hosts of others, necessary to the business, to become skilled in the construction of large ocean steamers and their machinery, and in their management, without practice? Yet, sir, in accordance with the progress of the age, the skill required for this business will become as necessary on the seas as railroads have already become to displace the mail coach and baggage-wagon on the land. I will here introduce a fact to show what difficulties have had to be encountered, and what large expenses incurred, in carrying out such an undertaking as the Collins line.

The main shaft of a large ocean steamer—a war steamer, if you please—was to be made: its length some thirty feet, more or less, and its diameter some twenty-four inches. You at once see that that was a huge mass of iron. For such a work we had no furnace of sufficient dimensions and capacity—they were altogether too small for such work. Our hammers were far too light; and our fires, while burning the surface of the metal, scarcely warmed the centre. Our best and ablest forgers were entirely unacquainted with the process of working such a huge mass of metal; and all, sir—all had to learn who undertook to do it—all had to learn by practice. Experiment on experiment failed, and resulted in consequent heavy losses, until, by costly improvements in the means, the artisan, by long and determined perseverance, had learned to perfect his work.

Mr. President, permit me to inquire who is to benefited by these experiments, these failures, these losses, this long perseverence, and this final success? The community is, or will be, as much benefited by them as those who achieved the success and paid the cost; and infinitely more so. And the Government—yes, sir, the Government—is, or will be, as much benefited as the community. And, sir, what I have said of this massive shaft is equally applicable to every portion of that huge machine—the marine engine—which propels the mammoth ocean steamer with such mighty speed across the Atlantic, and with which we have beaten the ablest mechanics and the best steamships and steam engines of the old world. And is this nothing to our Government? Is this nothing to the people of the United States?

Mr. President, the period is rapidly approaching when canvass will be a scarce article on the ocean, and when our steamers will constitute our navy. Then it will be found that whatever aid our Government may have extended to our merchant steam marine will not have been lost, inasmuch as, by that means, they will have enabled our mechanics and artisans to render invaluable aid, which they would not have been qualified to render without it.

Sir, the Government of the United States is emphatically dependent on the community for talent, ingenuity, and practical skill. They have no schools or other institutions for the purpose of mechanical instruction; and when ship-builders, engineers, or other mechanics are wanted, the Government, like an individual employer, must at all times be compelled to seek them where they are to be had. It is certainly, then, for the interest of the Government to foster those enterprises, by means of which the very talent and skill required for Government purposes may be the most readily developed and most properly disciplined.

In what school has been reared and qualified a race of the best seamen in the world, and among them a fair proportion of as bold and skilful navigators as ever trod a quarter-deck on the stormy Atlantic? Sir, that school is our eastern fisheries—a business that has long been fostered by the hand of the Government by the payment of large sums of money in the form of bounty; and these hardy denizens of the ocean have returned four-fold to their Government and their country for every dollar thus bestowed on them. Our great ocean steamers are rare schools for the purpose of turning out first-rate practical seamen, practical navigators, practical mechanics, and practical engineers; and I feel fully assured it is not affirming too much when I say there are no institutions in the United States in which all these professions—except perhaps those of the seaman and the navigator—can be studied to so great advantage, where practical knowledge of a high order can be so readily obtained, or where men can become so well qualified to discharge the duties of those professions, as on board those steamers. And, sir, is this nothing to our Government?—nothing to our country? Is it a matter of trivial importance to have our naval and merchant marine officered and manned by the best seamen, navigators, and engineers in the world? Is it a matter of no moment to this Government and this people to know that they have at their call mechanics who are capable of beating the world in the construction and equipment of ships, either for peace or war? Is it a matter altogether unimportant that, in case of war with a foreign nation, we can fill our ships with men reared in such a school, instead of those picked up here and there, without training, without experience, and without practical knowledge? Sir, I consider the question before the Senate as one that bears directly on this important subject. On its face it is a proposition to aid the Collins line of steamers, but, practically, I look upon it as one in which the Government and the country are deeply interested, for the reasons I have stated.

Mr. President, the honorable Senator from Virginia (Mr. HUNTER) has taken the ground that aid is in this instance, called for merely to enable the proprietors of the Collins line of steamers to keep up a ruinous competition with a foreign line, in a trial trip of speed on the ocean; and as the Collins line has not yet been able to sustain itself, he has come to the conclusion that it never can do so. Such being the case, he seems to think that, the sooner the business is given up to the Cunard line, the better. Further: he thinks also that, the business being a losing one, the more of it the Cunard line does, the sooner that line will be ruined. I do not think, sir, that the honorable gentleman, in coming to these conclusions, manifested his usual depth of thought, or clearness and force of argument. Sir, were these conclusions correct, and had a line of conduct been pursued in conformity with them with regard to our manufactures, not a yard of cloth, nor a ton of iron, would have been manufactured in this country. At first, and for a long time, it was a losing business in this country; and, to carry the honorable gentleman's conclusions out, our manufacturers ought to give the entire business to the foreign manufacturers at once, in order to involve them in speedy ruin.

Every one acquainted with the history of manufactures in this country well knows that those manufactures—especially that of iron, and that of cotton by machinery—were encouraged by bonuses and exclusive privileges, bestowed by the governments of the several States in which the were situated. Thus early did our ancestors deem it a matter of great public importance to encourage private enterprise for the public good. against foreign competition. But, sir, none of these enterprises were at first able to sustain themselves, even with the legislative patronage they received. One after another they all failed, and retired from the field of competition? And why was this? Simply because in this country the business was an untried experiment. It failed, as experiments, subsequently successful, frequently do at first, for the want of that skill which is to be acquired only by means of experience and practice.

Mr. President, suppose our manufacturers had finally adopted the conclusion arrived at by the honorable Senator from Virginia, and because their business had hitherto been a losing one given it up entirely into the hands of the foreign manufacturer, with the view of working his speedy ruin, what would have been the result? The foreign manufacturer would have retained the monopoly. He would have ruled our markets, and he would have exacted and extorted from us prices at least fifty per cent., and in many cases a hundred, above what we are now required to pay. To the fixed determination and indomitable perseverance of our mechanics, operatives, and manufacturers to compete with foreign skill, aided by protective duties, are due the invaluable improvements that have been made in all branches of manufactures, and the great reduction in prices that has taken place. This view of the subject in most of its bearings is equally applicable to the question now before the Senate.

In the enterprise of steam navigation on the ocean, Great Britain was many years ahead of us. Her first experiments were partial, and some of them total, failures. So have some of ours been, not excepting even some made by our Government. But by the time we had commenced in the same line of business, it had called to its aid in Great Britain the best scientific skill and knowledge in the world, and their powerful energies have been concentrated on the mighty work before them. After years of trial and toil they succeeded; and it was not till the proprietors of the Collins line had projected their gigantic enterprise that any attempt at all to be compared with that of the British company had been made in America. We had, to be sure, multitudes of steam engines, and fleets of steamboats, and few, very few, steamships; but among the whole there was no one to serve as a model or a guide for the construction and equipment of a steamship such as the object required or the nature of the contract with the Government demanded. Suppose the ships already built, there were no facilities adequate to the construction of their immense engines. All was to be created, sir, at an enormous expense of time, skill, and money—all was created. By long and determined perseverance the mechanical skill and ingenuity were found equal to the emergency. Practically the experiment has proved eminently successful. But so great has been its cost, and so powerful the rivalry, that hitherto it has not rewarded its projectors and proprietors as such a noble enterprise should. In this dilemma, the honorable Senator from Virginia advises those proprietors to relinquish the business to their rivals as the speediest means of bringing ruin on those rivals. We will examine this proposition.

Mr. President, to relinquish the Collins line would be precisely what the Cunard line particularly desires. To compel the Collins line to withdraw from its route is precisely what the Cunard line is attempting to do. Such a result once accomplished, and the business becomes a monopoly in the hands of the proprietors of that line. They can then have their own way, regulate prices to suit themselves, and not only sustain their line by means of their business, but enrich their company. To this end, together with a pride of feeling, they have formed the determination that no American line to rival theirs shall traverse the same route. True to this determination, and well knowing that the British Government will sustain them, they have adopted that petty species of competition which has long been practised to an extent injurious to all parties, and ruinous to some, between rival steamboats and stage coaches in this country. In other words, the British line has determined, cost what it may, to drive the Collins line from the ocean. The Collins line, or its proprietors, though strong in wealth, cannot compete with the Lords of the Admiralty, with the British treasury at their command; and the question is, as our neighbors on the other side of the Atlantic seem unwilling that we should run a line of steamers to one of their ports, whether we will or will not do it at any rate. To do it, sir, some further Government aid must be granted for the present. Without such aid, the enterprise must be relinquished, and we must be reduced to an absolute dependence on Great Britain for all the facilities required by the Government and the people of this country by means of steam navigation between our own ports and those of Great Britain. But, sir, the honorable gentleman does not believe it requires the aid asked for to enable the Collins line to go on. I need take up no more time in reply to this point than to say, and which is the fact, that the stock of the company can now be purchased in the market, in any quantity, at a discount of fifty per cent. from par. This simple fact will be, to every man at all acquainted with business, a full and sufficient reply to all argument based on calculation which may be intended to show that this line can continue in operation without the aid which this amendment is intended to afford. In order to show, sir, that the proprietors of this line and the citizens of New York wish for no monopoly, I am authorized to say that one million of dollars of the stock of the company will be sold at par, if wanted, to the citizons of any State in the Union, should this amendment prevail.

Mr. President, the honorable Senator from Virginia has characterized this competition as a mere trial of speed on the ocean. Sir, I have shown that it embraces much more than this. But, sir, no doubt this has had much to do with it; and, in my own opinion, the gratification of a high and honorable feeling of national pride is worth something to a Government and a country. Up to the period of the war of 1812 the American people had almost unanimously yielded their assent to the oft-reiterated boast that "Britannia rules the waves." That war afforded some practical data that cast some doubts on the legitimacy of the claim in a naval point of view. Our clipper ships have increased those doubts; and the superior speed of the little yacht America and our Collins steamers over any vessels of their description ever constructed in Great Britain has set the matter at rest. And can it be matter of surprise that the American people, who have been so long, constantly, and bitterly taunted by the English for their supposed inferiority in everything, should manifest some degree of national pride at these demonstrations? Is it not an amiable, patriotic feeling? It is not wonderful then, that they, the people, should expect, and, sir, they will expect, that some aid should be rendered to this line of steamers which, at such a heavy cost, and at so much loss, has achieved the greatest victory, whether of war or peace, that was ever achieved on the ocean—a victory, not of brute force, but of science and skill.

Mr. President, I ask if the Government and the country gain nothing by this enterprise? The vast improvements introduced by this company into steam machinery for sea-going purposes, and also into the vessels themselves, are invaluable, and worth more, vastly more, to the country than all the aid the company has heretofore received from the Government and that now solicited by them. Certainly such an enterprise does, on the score of the public good, demand some reward for all the sacrifices it has cost.

Sir, whether this line of steamers will or will not, with the aid now asked for, be able to sustain itself, is a question which time only can definitely answer. For my own part, I should think it would. The proprietors are good business men; and they, together with those engaged in managing and navigating these ships, will, of course, be learning every day, by means of practice, where improvements can be made and expenditures reduced; and, by a truly business-like and economical line of conduct, I believe the experiment will finally be found profitable, as it has most assuredly proved successful as to speed and safety. As an American citizen and an American mechanic, I feel, in common with my fellow-citizens, proud of the Collins line, and hope it may be sustained. Sir, I see no necessity for the apprehension expressed by the honorable gentleman from Virginia, that aid now rendered shall become a precedent for the future action of Congress. Congress will hereafter, as now, should such a question come up, act on the necessity, the justice, or the expediency of the case, without regard to precedent. These ships are partially in the employment of the Government—on them the Government has a lien—and, whenever the exigencies of the case may require, they will be converted exclusively to the Government service. Shall we, then, under such circumstances, withhold the aid required, and thus second the efforts of its foreign competitors to crush the enterprise at once, and thus deprive the Government and the country of the invaluable services of the finest and best line of steamships in the world? Sir, I hope not. It would mortify me, and so it would, I am certain, the great body of our citizens, to witness such a result. The honorable Senator, however, does not seem to look with a great deal of regret on the apprehended failure of the Collins line. Let it go down, he says, and by advertising we can have vessels as fleet as theirs, for a great deal less money. That the Government, by going into the market, and dickering, as the cant phrase is, with steamship owners, might obtain vessels for less money, is altogether likely; but whether equally fleet, is another question. They do not exist now, neither in this country nor any other. But, sir, the prudent man looks at the quality of an article as well as the price. You may procure vessels at much cheaper rates; but what will be their quality? You will not find those that have been built under the eye of the Government agent, and in accordance with the requirements of a Government contract. They may be good vessels. They may be safe vessels. Who will know, and who is to hazard the trial? Besides, sir, shall we exercise no magnanimity—no justice? True, sir, the Government has fulfilled the contract to its letter with this company, and paid all that was stipulated—all that was asked. But what then? Will the Government drive a hard bargain with its citizens; and, because they happened to make a miscalculation, compel them either to relinquish their contract, after having made enormous sacrifices in struggles for its fiulfillment, or to fulfil it at a sacrifice still greater. I trust not—I trust the Government has more magnanimity, more justice, more honor than to suffer such a result. I hope the aid to prevent it will be cheerfully afforded, and that this company will receive the encouragement and support they so richly merit.

But, sir, the honorable gentleman from Virginia went still further. He assumed that, in case the aid now asked for was granted, Congress would lie under obligation to extend similar aid, if required, to companies in any and every other port, formed for similar purposes. Sir, I cannot see the force of this argument. My own impression has been that Congress possessed some discretionary powers not exactly limited by precedents. The object in view in this case seems to me to test thoroughly our steam communication with England, the ablest mechanic power in the world, and in which attempt we necessarily come in competition with her own steamships, for the satisfaction and benefit of our whole country. By the result of this trial people in all the ports in our country will be ruled. Those who would wish to engage in this business are as much interested in having this experiment carried out as are the proprietors of this line. Should the experiment fail of success, then, of course it must be abandoned, and others would not be very ambitious to renew it. Should it succeed, no further aid would be required; and thus the people everywhere will learn the result without the further sacrifice of either private or public means. But there is still another important feature of the case to be considered.

Mr. President, can any other company come here under similar circumstances with those connected with the Collins line, and present similar claims? I believe not. The gentlemen constituting this company have invested in their noble steamers the amount of very nearly three millions of dollars. These ships have been regularly run at a continual heavy loss, in the fulfilment of the company's contract with the Government; and without some additional compensation for their services to the Government, their operations must cease, and the immense capital invested be very much impaired, if not lost. I believe it a case without a parallel in this country; and whenever another like it may come up here, it will be time enough to meet it. These facts would be sufficient to justify me in my own mind in voting for the relief asked for in this case; but I have others, if possible, more potent still. I refer, sir, to the contract between the Government and this company.

The Government required vessels of great strength and burden, capable of being converted into ships-of-war when required. The mail and passenger service required speed. Hence the company had to secure both objects. The ships are much heavier than would have been required for the mail and passenger service. Therefore they cost more than they world otherwise have done, required much heavier and more powerful engines, and are propelled and navigated at a much heavier expense. All these items combined make up the sum total of the extra expenses for which the appeal is now made to the justice as well as magnanimity of Congress. The proprietors of the line say, and I have no doubt truly, that, in building their vessels so much stronger and heavier than they would otherwise have done in carrying out their contract with the Government, and thereby incurring a greatly increased expense in constructing, equipping, and sailing, they acted in conformity with the wishes and instructions of the Navy Department. All this has been done by them in good faith; and after this, for them, in the face of a ruinous competition by a foreign line, sustained by a foreign Government, to be compelled to run their ships at a tremendous sacrifice to themselves, in the Government service, is, in my view, a flagrant violation of the principles of justice and equity.

Mr. President, during the discussion of this amendment, the amount paid per annum, or per trip, by the British Government to the Cunard line, has been stated and spoken of by way of comparison with the amount paid by our own Government to the Collins line. I have also made the statement, the truth of which will appear self-evident, that the cost of construction, equipment, and navigating the steamers of the Collins line had been greatly enhanced by reason of their excess of strength and tonnage over what would have been required for ordinary mail and passenger service alone. And the additional strength and tonnage were given to these vessels to fit them for war vessels. And, sir, I am now prepared to show, from the statement I hold in my hand, that the amount paid to the Collins line, will not be, all things considered, including what is contemplated in the amendment before the Senate, quite equal to the amount paid to the Cunard line.

The Cunard line has seven ships, the aggregate tonnage of which is 12,252 tons. These ships cross the Atlantic eighty-five times per year, or rather what is equivalent to eighty-five trips for one ship. This makes the total tonnage worked across the Atlantic, in the eighty-five trips, 148,750 tons. For this service they receive from the British Government, in round numbers, $856,820—making $5 75 per ton. The Collins line has four ships, of an aggregate of 13,702 tons, which cross the Atlantic fifty-two times per annum, or perform a service equal to fifty-two trips for one vessel. The amount to be paid by this amendment, and what is now paid, is

$858,000, or $4 82 per ton, and a fraction less than twenty per cent. below what is paid by the British Government to the Cunard line.

I have also a statement to which I desire to advert:

"In the London Times of the 10th of March occurs the following statement, which, though part only of it relates directly to the subject under consideration, we give entire for the benefit of such of our commercial readers as may feel an interest in looking over a complete table of the ocean mail service of Great Britain for the coming year:

"'The following table. partly compiled from a parliamentary paper, will show the estimate for the post office packet service for the coming year, as compared with that for the twelve months which will terminate on the 5th of April. The increase in the contracts last year was £98,135, and now we have a further augmentation of £64,862, caused chiefly by an enlarged allowance to the Cunard line for additional service, the extension of the West India contract to Brazil, and the establishment of new lines to Africa and Australia. On the other hand, there is a diminution of £4,200 in the expense of Queen's vessels employed; and the increase upon the aggregate total is therefore reduced to £60,662:

To and from--	Company.	Year.	
		1852-'3.	1851-'2.
Liverpool and Isle of Man..........	....	£850	£850
Holyhead and Kingstown..........	City of Dublin.........	25,000	25,000
Aberdeen and Lerwick..........	....	900	900
Southampton and Channel Islands..	S. W. Railway........	4,000	4,000
England and Hamburg, and England and Rotterdam............ ...	General Steam........	17,000	17,000
Southampton, Vigo, Oporto, Lisbon, Cadiz, and Gibraltar............	Peninsular and Oriental.	20,500	20,500
Liverpool and Halifax, and Boston and Liverpool, and New York....	Cunard..............	171,364	145,000
Halifax, Bermuda, and St. Thomas's, and Halifax and St. John's, Newfoundland....................	Cunard..............	14,700	14,600
Southampton and West Indies......	Royal Mail...........	240,000	240,000
Southampton, Brazil, and Buenos Ayres....................	Royal Mail...........	30,000	30,000
Callao and Valparaiso............	Pacific..............	25,000	25,000
Plymouth and Cape of Good Hope..	General Screw.........	30,730	30,730
England and West Coast of Africa..	Laird................	11,500	
England and Australia............	Australian...........	26,000	
England and Alexandria..........	Peninsular and Oriental.	22,500	23,000
Alexandria and Beyroot...........	Hall, Brothers.........	1,560	1,560
Suez and Calcutta, £115,000; less 7-16ths, payable by East India Company, £51,312............	Peninsular and Oriental.	64,688	64,688
Ceylon and Hong Kong, £45,000; less, as above £19,688..........	Peninsular and Oriental.	25,312	25,312
Bombay, (proportion paid to East India Company)..............	East India...........	50,000	50,000
Allowances of Government agents on board the contract packets........	....	10,683	9,285
		£792,287	£727,425
Expense of Queen's vessels employed in the packet service..........	....	77,871	82,071
Total expense..............	....	£870,158	£809,493

The Cunard line receives, it will be seen, for 1852 .	£171,364
While it received for 1851	145,000
Making an increase of	£26,364
Equal to	$131,820

The amount now received by the Cunard line is $856,820—being within less than $2,000 of what is asked for by Mr. Collins.

But, Mr. President, the honorable Senator from Virginia has said that these steamers were not fit for war steamers, as he had been informed by naval gentlemen, whose judgment was to be relied on. Well, sir, suppose this statement to be correct, it would weigh nothing in the argument. On the other hand, should these steamers prove the best war vessels in the world, their owners could not claim the credit of it. If they are totally unfit to be incorporated into the navy, it is no fault of theirs. They were built under the directions of persons appointed by the proper authorities to act for the Government. The company furnished the means, and the instructions from the Navy Department were carried out. If, then, the ships were to prove utterly worthless for war purposes, why should we blame their owners, and compel them to suffer the loss?

No. 1.

New York, *January* 19, 1848.

Sir: Having altered the dimensions of the mail steamers to be built by myself and my associates, as per contract dated 1st November last, under a law of Congress passed 3d March last, entitled "An act providing for the building and equipment of four naval steamers," I beg leave to wait on you with a specification for building the same, which I trust will meet your approval; and if so, you will please substitute it for schedule "A," now attached to the contract.

Yours, very respectfully,

E. K. COLLINS.

To Hon. J. Y. Mason, *Sec. Navy, Washington.*

No. 2.

Navy Department, Washington, *January* 26, 1848.

Sir: I received a letter dated at New York on the 19th instant, without signature, enclosing a "specification" for the building of the New York and Liverpool mail steamers for E. K. Collins and his associates. This paper being signed by yourself, it is presumed the communication was made by you. The subject has been referred to the Bureau of Construction for opinion, and, upon the recommendation of Commodore Skinner, the dimensions and specifications for building the mail steamers under the act of 3d March last, above referred to, are approved by the department.

I am, respectfully, your obedient servant,

J. Y. MASON.

No. 3.

New York, *February* 10, 1848.

Sir: Your letter of the 26th ult. was duly received. The unsigned letter, therein referred to, I hand you herewith, signed. My specifications for building the steamers, as mentioned in yours of the 26th, having been accepted, I am progressing in their building with as much speed as prudence dictates, watching strictly the interest of the Government and the owners, which interests I think inseparable.

I will thank you at an early day to appoint a naval constructor to superintend their construction in conformity to the law.

Yours, very respectfully,

E. K. COLLINS.

To Hon. J. Y. Mason, *Sec. Navy, Washington.*

No. 4.

Navy Department, *February* 14, 1848.

Sir: Your letter of the 10th instant, with the enclosure, has been received, and Captain Wm. Skiddy, of New York, has been appointed naval constructor for the purpose of superintending the construction of the steamers to be built under the act of Congress of March 3, 1847.

I am, respectfully, your obedient servant,

J. Y. MASON.

To E. K. Collins, esq., New York.

The contract referred to in the first of these letters contains the following:

"That whereas the said Collins and his associates submitted to the Postmaster General, on the sixth of March, Anno Domini eighteen hundred and forty-six, proposals to carry the United States mail between New York and Liverpool twice each month during eight months of the year, and once a month during the other four months, for the sum of three hundred and eighty-five thousand dollars per annum, payable quarter-yearly, and for this purpose proposed to build five steamships of not less than two thousand tons measurement, and of one thousand horse-power each, to be built for great speed, and sufficiently strong for war purposes."

Schedule A states the "intended size of said steamships about 3,000 tons."

In this connexion I will introduce the following:

Abstract of letters written by Commodore Perry and Captain William Skiddy, in reference to the Collins line of steamships, to the Secretaries of the Navy.

Commodore Perry, in his letter, dated February 18th, 1852, addressed to the Hon. William A. Graham, Secretary of the Navy, says:

"That the following-named Atlantic steamships may be converted, by slight alterations, into war-steamers of the first class—of Collins line, the Atlantic, Pacific, Arctic, and Baltic.

"According to my calculations, the cost of the conversion of either of the before mentioned vessels, exclusive of armaments, repair of machinery, &c., would not, or certainly ought not to cost for each steamer over $20,000, and it could readily be done for this at any of our navy yards. With respect to the description and weight of their respective armaments, I am clearly of the opinion that the first class steamers already named could easily carry four ten-inch Paixhan guns on pivots, two forward and two aft, of the weight of those in the Mississippi, and ten 8-inch

Paixhan guns on the sides, and this armament would not incommode the vessels and the weight less than the ice, which is usually forty tons, and stowed away in one mass."

Commodore Perry continues, and says:

"That in the general operations of a maritime war, they would render good service, and especially would they be useful, from their great speed, as despatch vessels, and for the transportation of troops, always capable of attack and defence, and of overhauling or escaping from an enemy.

"The Atlantic, Pacific, Baltic, and Arctic, have all been built, inspected, and received by the Navy Department."

Commodore Perry adds to this letter a note, and says:

"That an ocean steamer of 3,000 tons is of the maximum dimensions for safety and efficiency, whether for war or commercial purposes."

And this is the precise measurement of the Collins steamships.

In another note he says:

"That the best practical relative power of engines to tonnage for ocean steamers is one nominal horse power to every three tons of tonnage, custom-house measurement."

And this is the precise ratio of power used in the Collins steamships.

Commodore Perry, in his letter to the Hon. John Y. Mason, Secretary of the Navy, dated January 30, 1849, says:

"In accordance with my instructions from the department, I have carefully examined the vessels (Atlantic and Pacific) at present under construction and equipment, and in comparing them with the precise stipulations, I find some few deviations. The contract of E. K. Collins and his associates is in progress of completion. Two ships (the Atlantic and Pacific) are nearly ready, or quite ready for launching, and their engines and boilers are sufficiently advanced for commencing the work of putting them on board. As the contract with Mr. Collins does not refer to any particular vessel as a guide for a model or manner of construction of his ships, he has availed himself of the best material at command, and of his well known judgment and experience in ship-building, and in producing two very superior sea steamers."

Commodore Perry says, according to the statement of Captain William Skiddy, "that the ships are better fastened than was contracted for," and adds:

"The several contracts provide that all of these steamers shall be so constructed as to be easily converted into war-steamers, should the government exercise the right of taking them into their public service.

"Steamers are more easily armed than sail vessels, inasmuch as they have greater space on deck for pivot guns, possessing as they do greater facilities of motion, and consequent choice of position, and very little time would be required in arming and equipping them for war service."

Commodore Perry concludes this official statement as follows:

"The undertaking is one of great magnitude for individual enterprise, and of momentous character to the commercial interests of the country—an undertaking alike creditable to the liberal views of the Government and the public spirit of the contractors, and reflecting honor and credit upon both contracting parties.

"They (the steamships) will all have the merit of possessing the great essentials of capacity, buoyancy, and fleetness, and capability of carrying effective armaments; and if taken for their estimated worth at the time of the transfer, the Government will be the gainer, at a period of emergent want for such vessels."

Captain William Skiddy writes to "Commodore Perry, general superintending agent for the United States ocean mail steamers," on the 21st of January, 1849, as follows:

"I have received your communication of the 18th inst., requesting information respecting the construction and equipment of the United States mail steamers built and building in this port (New York) under my inspection.

"Mr. E. K. Collins' specifications and agreements with the Góvernment call for much less than has been executed, such as iron diagonal framing only one way; whereas they are double, crossing each other at right angles, and well bolted to timbers and riveted together; also the filling in amidships has been extended the whole length of the ships, with many other additions.

"These ships have great buoyancy, flat broad floors extended well forward and aft, with sharp ends, and are considered beautiful models. They have spacious deck room, and could carry guns of the largest calibre on the gun or middle deck.

"These ships can all, in case of emergency, be converted into fast war steamers. They would by law be received by appraisement on their original cost and their efficiency as to strength and materials; the necessary alteration included would cost the Government much less—perhaps one half of the amount required to build or purchase for the occasion.

"In case of a war, these are the only ships of sufficient strength and size in the United States that could be converted into war steamers."

Commodore Perry, April 9, 1850, writes to the Hon. W. B. Preston, Secretary of the Navy, thus:

"The models of the ocean mail steamers, built under the recent act of Congress, whether for the navy or mail service, may be considered as excellent.

"Experience has shown that the best general proportions for a war steamer with side-wheels are six times the breadth for the length and two thirds the breadth for the depth." (By a singular coincidence, this is the exact size of the Collins steamships)

"The highest probable speed that can with known machinery be given to commercial steamers of 1,500 tons, and carrying fourteen days fuel, and embracing an aggregate of voyages across the Atlantic, perhaps 10½ knots per hour has been the average.

"The aggregate of voyages across the Atlantic by the Collins steamships show that 12 knots per hour has been the average.

"The mail steamers of Howland & Aspinwall, and of E. K. Collins, esq., can be easily converted into war steamers.

"These vessels, with little strengthening of the decks, can be made to carry each a few guns of heavy calibre, and may be rendered useful to convoy and in the transportation of troops, &c. The use of steamships in our future naval operations must inevitably change in a great degree the art of naval war."

Captain Wm. Skiddy, on the 18th of February, 1852, writes to the Hon. Wm. A. Graham, Secretary of the Navy, thus:

"I herewith acknowledge your communication of the 10th instant to Com. M. C. Perry and myself, relative to the United States mail steamers built under contract with the Navy Department, and others carrying the mails of the United States.

"These ships (Atlantic, Pacific, Baltic, and Arctic) are not suitable for immediate war purposes, but can be made efficient in four or six weeks, and the cost of these alterations would not exceed for each ship $15,000 or $20,000. They would then be relieved of about one hundred and fifty tons weight, or nearly double the weight of guns and carriages, and would then have less resistance to water and wind, adding in increase to their already great speed."

The Hon. Wm. A. Graham, the present Secretary of the Navy, on the 20th of March, 1852, writes to the Hon. Wm. R. King, President of the Senate, in reply to a resolution for information in relation to contracts for the transportation of the mail by steamships between New York and California, on the Atlantic and Pacific oceans, as follows:

"It is respectfully suggested that a limited number of them, (steamships,) employed in time of peace in the transportation of the mails, would be found a most useful resource of the Government on the breaking out of war.

"In conformity to the standards required by these contracts, their readiness to be used at the shortest notice, their capacity as transports for goods and munitions of war, and their great celerity of motion, enabling them to overhaul merchantmen, and at the same time to escape cruisers, would render them terrible as guerillas of the ocean, if fitted with such armaments as could be readily put upon them in their present condition."

But, sir, what are the properties necessary for a war steamer? Speed is undoubtedly one. In point of speed what other seagoing steamers equal those of the Collins line? None, sir; none. They have beat the world and stand confessed without a rival on the ocean. The want of speed, therefore, cannot be among the supposed delinquencies of these ships. Great strength is another necessary property. Well, sir, I hazard nothing in saying the strength of no ship in the American navy has been so severely tested as the strength of these steamers. In gales of wind, when sailing vessels are lying to, and merely breasting the force of the waves, these ships are urging their way ahead with the mighty force of their powerful engines, perhaps at the rate of eight or ten miles per hour, and thus increasing the resistance, and consequent strain, to at least two-fold, compared with the sailing vessel. Yet, in this war of elements, they have never suffered.

Again, Mr. President: consider the enormous power of the engines by which these steamers are propelled. Each of these engines is of the calculated power of fifteen hundred horses, operating directly on the ship itself, as the fulcrum of the mighty lever by which she is driven through the waves. Every stroke of the piston is felt, sir, from stem to stern—from plankshear to keel—in every plank, in every timber, and in every fibre. Why, sir, one of these engines exerts a power sufficient to propel a ball of the weight of fifteen hundred pounds, with a velocity of thirty-three thousand feet per minute—a body which, taking the velocity into the account, would demolish the largest vessel that ever floated. The recoil of ten of the largest batteries in the world would not exercise so much strain on one of these steamers as does the power of her enormous engines. And yet, sir, with the buffeting of the waves, in gales and storms—with the exertion of all this propelling power—these gigantic ships, like the ocean rock amidst the waves, have withstood, unscathed and unshaken, some of the most terrible storms that agitate the Atlantic. Sir, what more perfect test can be given of strength, solidity, and seaworthiness than has been applied to these noble ships. For myself, I can conceive none.

But, sir, the honorable Senator now takes up another position. He says that propellers are superior to side-wheel steamers for war purposes. In this statement I perfectly agree with him, taking it as a general rule. But, sir, propellers would not answer the purpose of our Government for mail steamers. Their speed is not such as the times require. Under the Government direction, therefore, these steamers were equipped with side-wheels, and without which, however much they may take from their value and efficiency for war purposes, they would not have been available for the mail service. With the British or Cunard line the case is the same. However, sir, the honorable Senator admits we require some side-wheel steamers; and, sir, it fortunately happens that in the Collins line we have some—that is, we have four side-wheel steamers, the best in the world. The honorable Senator, however, regrets that the navy and the mercantile marine should be united at all. Sir, the honorable Senator's regrets come too late. As far as these steamers are concerned, it has already been done; and, in doing it, we have but copied the example of the greatest naval power in the world; and I am far from apprehensive that any evil will result from the act.

Mr. President, it does appear to me that not only pride of country, but also our mercantile interests demand that this line of steamers should not be left to an untoward fate without at least one more effort of this Government to prevent such a result. Sir, the war of 1812 cost this country three hundred millions of dollars. And for what was the war waged and prosecuted on our part? It was, sir, to secure our rights and promote our commercial interests on the ocean, and to cause them to be respected. The great object was gained; and, sir, as an American citizen, I thank Heaven that my country has never succumbed to a foreign power. Her flag still waves in all its glory, and is respected by every civilized nation on earth. Nor would I strike our flag of commerce. It has achieved a most important though peaceful victory, and I will not give my vote to have it furled, or struck to any foreign rival. But, sir, such must be the case should we refuse the aid contemplated in this amendment; and we must suffer the mortification of descending in the scale of commercial enterprise, and, for the want of some trifling pecuniary sacrifice, consenting to become second, when we were and might have remained first.

Sir, the superiority of our immense fleet of sailing vessels is already established. Foreign nations, with all their apparent superior advantages, have been unable to cope with us in this species of naval architecture. Our ships traverse every sea and unfurl our flag in every port in the world, and, wherever they appear, command the admiration of all observers. In this, our favorite and unequalled line of ocean steamers, we have also the evidence that we can excel, young as we are in this modern enterprise, all the rest of the world even in navigating the ocean by means of steam. To deprive us of this cause of triumph, and to prevent us from reaping its fruits, it is that those concerned in the British line have conspired to drive the ships of our American line from its route. This effected, and you suffer the spirit of enterprise concerned in the business to be crushed; and it will be a long time before it can again be aroused to action. On the other hand, encourage and sustain it, and but a few years will have elapsed ere we shall have a fleet of steamships traversing the ocean in ever direction, giving much greater facilities to commerce than it ever yet enjoyed, and greatly facilitating our communication with all parts of the world. Besides this, sir, our superiority in this matter being fully established, and universally known, as it will be, what is to prevent us from obtaining a large share of that lucrative business, now monopolized by Great Britain, of building steamships for other nations which lack the skill to build them for themselves? This would be extremely beneficial to our merchants and mechanics, and in fact to all classes in the community.

Mr. President, the increase of our steam-marine would also make heavy draughts on our immense coal fields. From

Ohio, from Indiana, from Kentucky, from Virginia, from Pennsylvania, and wherever coal is found, it may be transported to all our seaports, from Portland to New Orleans, and at every port it would meet with a ready sale. If all these interests are of any importance in our view, let us unite to promote them by lending a helping hand to the company which solicits it, and whose noble ships, I trust, are destined to become the nucleus of a numerous fleet, all equally excellent.

Mr. President, I cannot permit myself to close these remarks without paying a well-merited compliment to the gentlemanly proprietors of the celebrated Collins line of steamers, equalled by none that float on the bosom of the ocean. Sir, these gentlemen certainly deserve well of their country. With a degree of munificence seldom equalled they have expended their money without stint on an object truly national, and by the result have placed our country ahead of all others, in point of practical success, with respect to steam navigation on the ocean, and thus wrested the palm of victory from the brow of that mighty naval power which has claimed for centuries to be the mistress of the seas. More than this, sir: the millions they have expended, and by which they have not profited themselves, have gone to reward honest industry and mechanical science and skill. They have probably in this way done more for the working portion of the community and the cause of steam navigation than a like number of men in the same length of time have ever done before in the United States; and, whatever may be the ultimate fate of their enterprise, on which they have expended so much money, they are now honored, and will long be remembered with honor, for their noble work—a work that has opened a new era in the history of steam navigation, the effects of which will be seen and felt for generations yet unborn.

SPEECH

OF

HON. SOLON BORLAND,

OF ARKANSAS,

AGAINST THE COLLINS LINE OF STEAMERS,

AND AGAINST

SPECIAL LEGISLATION—THE DOCTRINE OF PROTECTION—AND ALL MONOPOLIES.

DELIVERED

IN THE SENATE OF THE UNITED STATES,

MAY 12 AND 17, 1852.

"Beginning with the first charter of the United States Bank, and ascending through the whole series of minor monsters and monopolies to this model contract with the Collins line, vary its aspect, and disguise it as you will, the principle you violate is the same, and the evil you do is of the same general character, only less or more in proportion to the degree of force you move it with. This is—it must be so, if God governs his universe by laws."—*Page* 19.

WASHINGTON:
PRINTED AT THE CONGRESSIONAL GLOBE OFFICE.
1852.

SPEECH.

The Senate resumed, as in Committee of the Whole, the consideration of the bill from the House of Representatives entitled "An act to supply deficiencies in the appropriations for the service of the fiscal year ending the 30th of June, 1852," the pending question being on the amendment of the Committee on Finance, as it had been amended, to insert the following:

For additional compensation for increasing the transportation of the United States mail between New York and Liverpool, in the Collins line of steamers, to twenty-six trips per annum, at such times as shall be directed by the Postmaster General, and in conformity to his last annual report to Congress, and his letter of the 15th of November last to the Secretary of the Navy, commencing said increased service on the first of January, 1852, at the rate of $33,000 per trip, in lieu of the present allowance, the sum of $236,500: *Provided*, That it shall be in the power of Congress at any time after the first day of January, 1854, to terminate the arrangement for any additional allowance herein provided for.

Mr. BORLAND said:

Mr. PRESIDENT: It was not my wish or intention to speak at all upon this deficiency bill, further than to vote ay or nay upon the various items which compose it, as they might be severally submitted to the Senate. And if others, on both sides of the Chamber, had not debated it at such length, and in such a way as some have done, I should certainly now remain silent. But the discussion has been so extended and elaborate, and especially the amendment in favor of the Collins line of ocean steamers, now under consideration, has been advocated by its friends so urgently and upon such grounds, that I deem it a duty, which I owe to myself and those I represent, to record my views on the other side.

In thus recording what I call my views, it is not because they *are my* views, and mine alone, that I wish to declare them. Such a reason could not—could never, indeed—induce me to occupy the time of the Senate. But it is because I believe those views are, in the first place, founded upon *facts;* and, in the second place, are in accordance with those principles of legislation and those maxims of political economy which have so long been held to be sound and sacred by the political party to which I belong. And, further, because I have not found those principles and maxims sustained, on this occasion, by some of those under whose lead I have heretofore been accustomed to contend for them—some whose fortune and whose pleasure it has heretofore seemed to be to stand in the forefront of the battle in their support—some whose duty and whose interest I had trustingly hoped would hold them alike to the faith they had so long and so ably taught, and to the good works their practice had so uniformly and brilliantly exemplified. On the contrary, by some of these, those views have been opposed. I do not mean by this that *no one* in this discussion has sustained the principles and the maxims I espouse. I could not mean that, while the honorable Senator from Virginia [Mr. HUNTER] is in my eye, and especially while the ability and eloquence with which he has resisted this appropriation are so fresh and glowing in my memory. And there have been other honorable Senators, newer on this theater, who have come to the rescue, and done good service on the same side. From their political associations I had not hoped this of them. But a sense of patriotism, superior to that of mere party, has lifted them above the barrier of those associations, and brought them, battling, to the cause of right, and that, too, when the odds are against her; when, alas, *right* is not *might* upon this field. I honor them for it. Would that we could always have them with us.

What the Senator from North Carolina [Mr. BADGER] said of the Senator from Virginia, [Mr. HUNTER,] in this connection the other day, was well deserved. It is, indeed, true, "that if in number he is but one, in force he is a host." I will not say his valor or his prowess was exaggerated by comparing him with "Achilles upon the plains of Troy, driving whole battalions before him." But, as my honorable friend [Mr. BADGER] has sought classic ground for similitudes, I would suggest that he need not have stretched his fancy so far back into the regions of antiquity as to disturb the mythical shades of a mythical poet's demigods. An apter comparison, I apprehend, might be found in the annals of more reliable history some six hundred years later, when that Spartan, whose name has come down to us as the synonym of firmness and devotion, stood almost alone in the famed pass of Thermopylæ. And, perhaps, this comparison might appear the more striking and appropriate were it extended a little further. For it does seem clear to my mind that if *every Greek* had but proved true to Leonidas, the Persians could never have prevailed. The repulse of their onslaughts for three succesive days had driven them back, conquered and desponding; and, in my opinion, they never would have renewed the attack while, with the mountain barriers of the Constitution on his right hand and the deep sea of good policy on his left, the bold front and trenchant blade of our gallant chief had continued to occupy that "twenty-five feet of ground" over which, *alone*, by a forward movement of the enemy, the heart of his country could be reached. But, alas! sir, for the supremacy of constitutional legislation and sound political economy "in the middle of the nineteenth century," as for Grecian independence more than two thousand years ago, there has ever been such a thing as stratagem in politics as in war—back ways of approach to an American Congress, as there were secret "mountain passes" to the rear of the Spartan camp. Sir, we are surrounded—we are beaten! I not only see before me the interminable lines of our natural enemies, but I hear in close proximity, and with painful distinctness behind me, the tramp of some heavy cohorts we had always deemed our friends, now acting in concert with the *five millions* of Persians which Xerxes leads againt us. Ay, sir, we are attacked in front and rear. And you are aware, Mr. President, that in politics as in war, it is a fearful hazard to be attacked in front and rear at the same time. You remember how even the tried valor of General Scott quailed at its contemplation when he went to Mexico. And it is very certain that such an attack, as planned by Santa Anna, had it been executed by Miñon, would have beaten General Taylor at Buena Vista.

I repeat, sir, we are surrounded and beaten. I see it all—I feel it—I know it. And since, in lamenting this calamity, I have been tempted by the example of my classical friend over the way, [Mr. BADGER,] far back into the shadowy land, for incidents of comparison, he, at least, must bear with me while I linger there, to find some likeness of myself to the faithful *Eurytus;* for if, like him, in conscious weakness, I have bided at *Alpenus*, and kept aloof from my gallant chief while the enemy were all in front, and he seemed able, with his single arm, to beat them off and drive them back; yet, now that he is surrounded, and evidently doomed to fall, I, too, have left that position—whence, from "the loop-holes of retreat," I might have watched the battle from afar, in silence and in safety—and hasten to his side in that hour, when, if I cannot bring him aid to win a triumph, I may, at least, share with him the martyrdom and glory of defeat. For, sir, intuitive and strong as are my likings for a *majority*—and in this I am every inch a Democrat—yet, with the principles of Democracy I have learned, in part, at least, from you and the distinguished Senator from Michigan, [Mr. CASS,] who sits behind me, (but should always be before me,) and which I have ever professed and practiced, I would infinitely prefer to record my name upon your Journal as the *single one* of a forlorn minority against this measure, than to be the foremost man of the heaviest majority in favor of it, which that Journal could be made to bear. *Amicus Plato, amicus Socrates, sed magis amica veritas!*—an appropriate version of which noble sentiment I adopt, in strong, terse old English, from the proud avowal of that great American heart, no longer here to electrify a listening Senate, but a little way hence, paling its fires before the light of another world, and stilling its mighty pulses on the margin of an honored grave—

"I HAD RATHER BE RIGHT THAN BE PRESIDENT!"

—A sentiment, sir, to which no heart bows with a deeper reverence than mine, but which might fall with far more fitness and significance, on this occasion, from other lips.

Such, Mr. President, is the spirit which actuates me—such the purpose which engages me in this discussion.

In the execution of this purpose, it is not at all necessary, nor shall I undertake, to occupy the whole ground of dispute, or consider every point of interest it presents. This has already been sufficiently done, and well done, by the honorable Senator from Virginia, [Mr. HUNTER,] whom I have acknowledged as my leader on this occasion. I shall content myself, therefore, with touching a few of the main points upon which the decision of the whole question turns; and even so much, not with the slightest expectation of influencing a single vote, nor with even the shadow of a hope of turning any man's mind from the fixedness of present determination. This is another case, and it is likely to be *a memorable one*, of "foregone conclusion." I speak, therefore, for the sole purpose of placing the reasons of my own vote upon the record, and that my constituents may see that in this instance, as I trust in all others, I have, however feebly, yet faithfully, represented their principles and their interests, by asserting my own.

The original ground upon which the first appropriations were asked and advocated for this line of steamers, and the only one upon which their advocates seemed then to rely with any confidence, was the adaptation of the vessels to "war purposes"—ay, sir, that was the term—"war purposes;" and their incorporation, as the most important element, alike for economy and efficiency, into our system of naval armament and defense. We all well remember how earnestly and confidently this was urged and insisted upon, as a consideration in its behalf; and no one, I apprehend, will question or deny that it was the consideration which secured a majority in its favor, and determined the success of the proposition. Upon that ground, alone, I hesitated, and was some time in doubt, whether I should support or oppose it. My instinctive aversion to all monopolies, to class legislation in every form, and under whatever specious guise it might present itself, and to all partnerships between the Government and speculators in patriotism, made me suspicious of it at the first, and I was disposed to reject it without much examination. But there I was met with this attractive and captivating phrase of "war purposes." I confess it was very attractive and captivating to my fancy. I had but recently returned from Mexico; and although a year and a half in that interesting country—one third of the time a prisoner of war—had somewhat abated my military ardor, yet it had not "taken the starch quite out" of me. The very name of "war," and the means of its successful prosecution, bore then a spell of power to me, as now, I doubt not, they do to the martial spirit of the honorable Senator from Michigan, [Mr. CASS,] which I found it difficult, as it now seems impossible for him, to resist. But not only did *this* attract. I was reminded of the wonders which steam, as a motive power, had already worked in commerce and the arts; and was pointed to the future, for the still greater triumphs it was to achieve in arms. The past I was bound to admit—the future I could not contradict. I was, further, reminded of our expensive naval establishment, which apparently, or at least comparatively, useless, though scarcely less expensive, in our long intervals of peace, was growing into a subject of complaint with a portion of the people. This I knew to be so. Then, by what seemed a very natural transition, the importance of our Atlantic mails, and the good policy of having them regularly, and speedily, and economically transported back and forth across the ocean, were suggested and enlarged upon—I will not say exaggerated, but certainly they were not estimated at less than their true value. The array, so far, was attractive, and imposing, and formidable—certainly so to one like myself, fresh from a region where such things were not familiar, and new to the business and appliances of national legislation. But one more element was needed to make the demonstration complete. That was speedily supplied; and the solution was before me—as clear in its terms, as accurate in its letters, and as precise in its lines and angles, as I, when a school-boy, and "crammed for an examination," had ever made, to blunder through *pons assinorum*, on the black board. *Eureka!* exclaimed the kind and skillful Palinurus, who had conducted me so far into these strange seas, as he opened to my astonished and delighted vision the fair harbor of New York, crowded with the Collins steamers, each one freighted with mail-bags for all Europe, and embrazured with guns to whip the world in arms! Here, I was told, was to be found a panacea for all the ills complained of, in the way of a useless and expensive naval establishment, alike, in peace and war, and of deficient mail service; and which, at the same time, would prove the very nursery and handmaiden, *par excellence*, of science, literature, commerce, and the mechanic arts. The Senator from New Hampshire, [Mr. HALE,] had not then added, as he did the other day, civilization, morality, and religion, to the catalogue of its blessings, present and prospective. This panacea—this wonder-working, and good-compelling instrumentality—when disclosed, was neither more nor less than to advance Mr. Collins money to build his ships, and when they should be built, to pay him for transporting in them our mails from New York to Liverpool.

A distinguished medical professor once said of Crawford's (since Liebig's) combustion hypothesis of animal heat, that "if the facts which served as a foundation for this beautiful theory, were not false, the deductions would be irresistible." Some such defect, it occurred to me, there possibly might be, in this hypothesis of the Collins line. For I was not, as I am not now, without suspicion that there are such things as "false facts" in commerce, steamships, and speculation, as well as in the experimental science of chemistry. Upon this suspicion I paused, and I also examined the question—imperfectly and with difficulty, I admit, yet with the best lights before me, and surely with an earnest wish to ascertain the truth. It is not necessary to trouble the Senate with the whole process of that examination. It is enough, for my present purpose, to say that it failed to satisfy me that the positions assumed were facts established, or that the promises made either would be or could be performed. So I adhered to my original principle of action, and opposed the contract and appropriation. And what has the result proved? It may be said, I know, that time enough has not been yet allowed to make a full trial of the experiment. Be that as it may, this I do know, and all the country knows, what indeed is proved by the very presence of this proposition here before us at this time, that, in every material particular, the experiment has failed—utterly failed—upon its original conditions. The steamers for *war purposes* were to be built, but they have not been built; the efficiency of our Navy was to be increased, but it has not been increased; the expenses of our naval establishment were to be reduced, but they have not been reduced; the cost of transporting our Atlantic mails across the ocean were to be paid by the revenues from this line; but, instead of that, we have not yet received back quite one dollar for the three paid out. In a word, all this service of curing evils and securing good was to be rendered for the amount of money then appropriated, but it has not been done; so far from it, indeed, that here before us we have the broad confession of the fact of the failure, in the demand from the same parties, for nearly double the amount of compensation; and we are coolly told, that unless we choose to give it, the experiment will fail and be abandoned, and all we have heretofore intrusted to the science, and skill, and enterprise, and patriotism of this company, to be expended for the promotion of the public interest, and to sustain the national honor, will be a dead loss. Such a demand, from such a source and under such circumstances, argues, to my mind, one or the other of two propositions: either that the parties making it are afflicted with a grievous inability to appreciate the relations of cause and effect, or that they are gifted with a still more remarkable shrewdness of reliance upon the facility with which Congress yields to demands boldly made, and pertinaciously pressed upon us. The result, alone, will prove whether Mr. Collins and his associates shall hereafter lay their grateful votives upon the altars of dullness or sagacity.

I have not given the items of the account upon which I have based my general statement of results, and from which I have drawn my general conclusions. They have been already and sufficiently given, by the honorable Senator from Virginia, [Mr. HUNTER,] who, in the performance of his duty as chairman of the Committee on Finance, has thoroughly investigated this subject in its details, and laid the facts before us. I need not weary the Senate by recapitulating them. It is enough, for my purpose, that they are before us, and before the world. I rely upon them, and feel perfectly well satisfied that they warrant every inference I have drawn from them. I may, in publishing my remarks, incorporate or append some of them, in the form of extracts and tables.

I have assumed that the element of "war purposes," however potentional it may have been in the original problem, never was legitimately there; and even if it had been, yet, in the course of the demonstration, it has been left out as incongruous and impracticable. The exposition made by the Senator from Virginia [Mr. HUNTER] rendered this fact indisputable. But, sir, even if that were not so, it has been proved so clearly, and significantly, and conclusively, by the honorable Senator from North Carolina, [Mr. BADGER,] that I cannot suppose it will ever be seriously insisted on again. That Senator, a friend, too, to this appropriation, and as well informed upon these subjects as any gentleman upon this floor—always excepting, of course, the honorable Senator from New Jersey, [Mr. STOCKTON,] on my left—has proposed to amend the bill, by cutting all, even seeming connection, between this line and the Navy, and turning them over, bodily, to the Post Office Department.

The Senator withdrew his proposition; but he had made it.

Mr. BADGER. I am still in favor of it.

Mr. BORLAND. I have no doubt of it; and for that reason, were there no other, I attach importance to it. But, sir, not only has the Senator from North Carolina done so, but the Senator from Texas, [Mr. RUSK,] in his place here yesterday, cut that connection, even more abruptly and completely than the Senator from North Carolina proposed to do. And how? In the course of an incidental debate upon the proposition of the Senator from Florida, [Mr. MALLORY,] he spoke of the connection between the Navy and this line of vessels as "seeming, and seeming only;" and that its expenses ought not to be set down to the Navy account. Yes, sir, the connection, he said, between the two was "seeming, and seeming only."

Mr. RUSK. I stated distinctly, and I have done so before, that no reasonable, intelligent man, could charge the expenses of these ocean mail-steamers to what is termed the Navy proper. I have expressed that idea on more than one occasion. So far from holding the position that these are not sufficient war vessels, I maintain now that they are; and not to trespass further upon the Senator, when he asks who says these vessels are capable of being war-steamers? I tell him Captain Skiddy and Commodore Perry; and he is entitled to the benefit of my opinion, for I believe they are better than any vessels in the Navy.

Mr. BORLAND. I do not question that such is the opinion of the Senator on that subject. He has declared it over and over again, and the whole country knows it. I alluded to his statement upon an incidental proposition here yesterday, when he admitted the impropriety of having this appropriation, or any part of the expenses of this line, connected with the Navy fund, or with the Navy in any respect; declaring that this connection was "seeming, and seeming only." But I ask any intelligent man, if these are ships of the Navy, capable of being used for war purposes, where is the impropriety of charging the money for sustaining them to the naval appropriations? It seems to me that would be the most natural connection in the world; and with whatever ease a person practiced in examining the accounts of the different branches of our public service, might be able to determine that this money was not properly charged to the naval appropriation; yet, I apprehend, it would go out to the country as the strongest declaration, which nineteen-twentieths of the American people who saw it, whether intelligent or not intelligent, would take as evidence that this line was a part of the Navy, and that this sum was a part of the naval appropriations, and properly so.

Mr. President, it seems that, not only is this opinion entertained of this matter by the Senators to whom I have alluded, and by myself; but you remember that yesterday, when the vote was taken upon the proposition of the Senator from Florida, there was almost a tie vote in the Senate upon it; and there is no question, in my opinion, that in a full Senate the present connection would have been severed, and the whole transaction would have been stamped, as it deserves to be, as a Post Office arrangement, and nothing more. I therefore assume this to be a fact, satisfactory to my mind at least, and I think fully sustained by the evidence before us. I think the proposition of the Senator from North Carolina was right, as it was significant. It carried with it an important explanation, which I think it is time the American people had before them. It was straight-forward and intelligible. At any rate, I think it placed the thing in its true position before the Senate. It stripped the daw of its borrowed plumage. It let the gas out of the balloon; and gave to the speculators' "airy nothing" of "war purposes" its true name and "local habitation." There, for the present, I leave it.

The whole proposition, then, to my mind, is to establish and maintain a mail-line across the Atlantic ocean. To that proposition, in itself, I have no objection. Indeed, I am in favor of it—as much so, I apprehend, as any Senator upon this floor, or any citizen of this country. But the question is—How shall we establish and maintain such a line?

In answering this question practically, it is well to consider how the other portions of our mail system are arranged and conducted, how the lines are established, how the service is procured, how it is performed, and how it is paid for.

By our general law, all navigable waters are declared to be mail routes; and, by occasional laws, certain roads upon the land are, also, declared to be mail routes. To establish lines, or, in other words, to put service, or have the mails carried, upon the routes which have been established by law, is in the power, and at the discretion, within certain limits, of the Post Office Department. When, in the judgment of that Department, the public interest requires it, these lines are established, and their service procured. As the law now prescribes, and as I trust it always will prescribe, public advertisement, giving due notice, is made throughout the country, inviting proposals for carrying the mails; the contract to be awarded to the lowest and best bidder. Formerly—I think until 1845—the advertisements specified the means and mode of service, as well as the time, the route, and the distance; and the contracts were made to conform to that specification. Since that time, the simple act of service, conditioned only as to time, route, and distance, is alone provided for; the means and mode of transportation being left to the contractor. This change was not made without cause, or without reflection. I thought, at the time, it was a wise and a proper change; and I also think the result has proved it to have been so. For, there is nothing more clearly and fully established than the fact, that, while the mail service, generally, has been as well and efficiently performed—perhaps better—the rate of its cost has been very greatly reduced. To prove this, we need only refer to the annual reports of the Post Office Department, before and since the change. There was another reform in the same connection, and the same time; and that was to abandon the requirement which had, up to that time, been made of the new contractor, to purchase of the old one, all his old and worn-out "stock"—that is, horses, coaches, &c., which he might have on hand, however worthless it might be, at the close of the old and the beginning of the new contract.

I well remember the great reduction in the rate of cost of mail-service, from these two items of reform, set forth in his report, by the Postmaster General, in 1846. He assigned the saving from these items, alone, as a very considerable resource, if not the main one, which had sustained the Department, in any tolerable degree, under the sudden and very great reduction of the rates of postage by the act of 1845.

These changes, proper and useful as they were, in point of financial economy, were, in my opinion, still more proper and more useful, by repudiating the principle and abolishing the practice of an interference by the Government, any further than may be indispensable to the public interest, in the business of the country, or of its undertaking to regulate, except by general laws, the ordinary transactions between private individuals. All the Government wanted, and all it could legitimately ask, was the performance of certain service—the transportation of the mail over certain routes, within certain times—and for this to pay a certain sum of money, the smallest sum for which this would be undertaken, by some competent and responsible man, binding the contractor, in sufficient bonds, to perform his contract faithfully, and so supervising the service, in the course of its performance, as to secure the public interest from detriment. This done, the duty of the Government was performed, and its functions ceased, in that direction. Further than this it could not legitimately go, and, in my opinion, should never be permitted to go. I think the history of our Government shows that whenever, by itself, it has undertaken to perform the functions of private individuals, there has always been a failure to perform those functions well; and especially has this failure been manifest, and most mischievous in its consequences, whenever, by special legislation and time-serving policy, the Government has undertaken to provide for and regulate the business of the country—business which should be left where it properly belongs, to be suggested by the sagacity, pushed forward by the enterprise, and managed by the enlightened self-interest of the citizen himself. All history, I think, teaches us that this has been so; and that it will ever be so in all time to come, is no less the suggestion of reason than it is the admonition of experience.

Upon this idea, a saying of Nathaniel Macon, who once honored the Senate with his presence, and guided it by his wisdom, may be quoted here, as an apposite and instructive exemplification. I heard it attributed to him here a few years ago, by a Senator no longer a member of this body. "*If*," said Mr. Macon, "*the Government of the United States should undertake to become a farmer, it would, before the end of five years, have to buy its corn for planting.*" That, sir, presents the very *beau ideal*, or, in the language of the day, the *daguerreotype*, of an incompetent and unthrifty farmer.

So, sir, it has ever been, and so it will ever be, whenever the Government has left, or shall leave, the sphere of its legitimate functions, to interfere in the affairs of the people, or undertake the performance or regulation of duties which individual men should perform, and which they alone, when left to themselves, can properly and efficiently perform.

This has been so with the mails. Mr. Macon said it would be so with the crops, and I believe it. And so, Mr. President, I think it ever has been, and feel sure it ever will be, in every pursuit in life, and with every article or fabric of production.

Look, sir, at the planting of corn, and of cotton, and of tobacco, and of sugar, and of hemp! What does this Congress know of those pursuits, or of those productions, which is not far better known to those individuals whose intelligence is sharpened by an interest we cannot feel, whose knowledge is enriched by observations we have no opportunities to conduct, and whose judgment is matured by an experience not attainable by us, nor in the habitual channels of our thoughts and occupations? Why, then, should we interfere with them? Why undertake, by special legislation, to prescribe the manner in which those crops shall be cultivated, or the quantity of each which shall be produced, or how they shall be carried to market, or at what prices they shall be sold? All those things should be left, as, thank God, they have been left, to the practical intelligence, the ample knowledge, the mature judgment, of the men whose interest it is to regulate them wisely. The result has been, good management and thrift, under the salutary laws of demand and supply; and the inevitable consequence is a prosperity as glorious as it is unexampled.

Then look at the various manufactures of the country! What do we know of them which is not far better known, or what can we do for them which cannot be far better done, by the practical minds and hands which are engaged in their management and identified with their success? The same principles of human action, and the same general laws of business and of trade, apply here and determine results, as in agriculture, as I have mentioned. Unfortunately for manufactures themselves, unfortunately for the country, and, at one time, almost to the ruin of this Government, the same wisdom has not, in every instance, presided over our national councils; or, at any rate, if she did preside, she sadly verified what was said of her predecessor in remote antiquity, that wisdom "sometimes nods." For if we did not directly interfere with manufactures, to the extent of prescribing the several processes of spinning and weaving, or of directing, in so many words, the precise quantity and quality and price of production, we did what, perhaps, was in equal disregard and violation of principle, and what, in the end, proved even more mischievous in practice, when, by special legislation, at the expense of every other interest of the country, we administered a stimulus to manufactures of certain classes, which, while it excited them to temporary excesses, alike of investment and production, was yet insufficient to protect them adequately against foreign or domestic competition, or place them upon a secure and permanent foundation; and with what consequences to those manufactures themselves? Need I remind Senators of what almost every page of our legislative history discloses? Who does not know? What student of that history has not dwelt with interest, and felt his heart throb with alternate fear and hope, as he traced the rise and progress of the protection I allude to, during that stormy period of thirty years, from 1816, when it began, until 1846, when it was last the wager of a battle which shook these walls? If the time were at my disposal, it would be of interest, and might be instructive, to pass, in review, all the leading incidents which make up that history. It may, under present circumstances, however, only be admissible, and will be enough for my purpose, to refer to a few of them only.

Except that it has been cited as a precedent, and has furnished some color for subsequent abuses, I do not say that I find objections to the tariff act of 1816. The circumstances under which it was enacted, and the reasons which governed its authors, I have ever thought justified it at the time. We were then in our infancy as a nation, (as I was in mine as an individual.) Our resources were limited. We had just emerged from a harassing and expensive war, with the most powerful nation in the world; with our patriotism purified by blood and fire, and aroused to its full strength and ardor; with our hatred of England and everything English intense and concentrated; and with our hearts open and warm to all who had given us sympathy and assistance in our days of trial, and were here to rejoice with us in our hour of triumph. We wanted revenue to relieve us from the burden of a debt, which was the price of our second independence, as well as to defray the expenses of a Government whose power and value had now begun to be felt. Our people were galled and exhausted by the direct taxation, which had been onerous during the war. Relief was desired and needed, in all quarters. If ever there was, or could be, an occasion in the career of any people, when a resort to duties upon imports, for the means of relief and support was presented, indeed forced upon them, it was our occasion in 1816. But in addition to this general consideration, which was scarcely less than a necessity, the few manufactures then in our country had arisen, and were then placed, under very peculiar circumstances. They had arisen during the war, fostered and encouraged by the non-intercourse, and comparative isolation, which war with a maritime power had imposed upon us. And not only had these manufactures been thus fostered and encouraged, but they had rendered important, indispensable services, by supplying our wants during those dark days of isolation, and suffering, and danger. In view of their condition, then, and especially in consideration of the indispensable services they had rendered in our time of need, there was not only a sense of good policy in the minds of our public men of that day, which suggested this mode of raising revenue, but there was also a sentiment—and a worthy sentiment it was—of gratitude in the hearts of all, which conceded protection to our infant manufactures. And to appreciate fully the need they had of some protection, it must be borne in mind, that not only were they immature and feeble in themselves, but that, during the war, there had accumulated in various European countries, especially in England, large stores of manufactured goods which awaited but the hand of peace to remove the barriers which war had erected, to pour their floods upon our shores, at prices reduced by excess of quantity, and thus to sweep our friends from the face of our own soil. Such is my reading of the history of the tariff of 1816, and such the considerations for which, I apprehend, I should have sustained it, had I been here to vote.

But, sir, as I said, the circumstances of that occasion were peculiar. The mere recital of them proves that they have not occurred, and never can occur again in our history. With the occasion, then, which originated and justified the policy of protection, the policy itself must cease and determine. And here, sir, that I may avoid all chance of being misapprehended, or of being suspected of inconsistency upon this point of *protection*, I must remind all who hear me of what that protection in 1816 consisted. The rate of the duties then imposed, I cannot now, from memory, state with precision. I am quite sure, however, that it did not exceed thirty per cent. *ad volorem*. But, at any rate, it did not exceed the rates of our revenue tariffs since that time; and in itself was entirely within the revenue limit of its day. My impression is, that it averaged about twenty-eight per cent.

But, Mr. President, that was the beginning; and though, like that apple which "brought death into the world, and all our woes," it was harmless in itself, and even pleasing to the taste, from that time dates, and from that has sprung, innumerable woes in our world of politics. It may be in accordance with human nature, for it certainly followed, that what was first received as bounty and protection, was soon demanded as a right; and that, too, by parties who had not even earned the first bounty! The poet has said that

> "Fools rush in
> Where angels fear to tread."

I need hardly express the analogy which the demands of this second class of claimants for protection suggest to my mind. If I did, it would be, that

> Knaves are clamorous for gain,
> Where honest men would hold their peace.

But the demand was made, and pressed with a zeal and in a spirit of such sturdy beggary, that it seemed to defy alike refusal and resistance; and had attained its height of exorbitancy and success in 1828. The tariff act of that year was not inaptly characterized, at the time, as "the bill of abominations." You were here, Mr. President, and know all about it. I was still a boy—though not even then altogether uninformed, and certainly not indifferent, as to what was passing of a nature so important to the welfare of my country, and so generally agitating the minds of the people.

Pardon me, sir, for these reminiscences. They are of deep interest to me; being, of that period of my life, when my political opinions may be said to have had their birth—or, at least, to have taken their indelible impression from "the form and pressure of the times." And in this connection, I trust the honorable Senator from North Carolina, [Mr. MANGUM,] who sits furthest from me, will not object that I refer to him for the state of popular sentiment in the good old State, which he still so ably represents; for those were stirring times, sir, and that honorable Senator was among the foremost of those strong spirits who stirred them—and that, too, *against* "*abominations.*" I, then a boy—perhaps not older than the youthful Norval, when martial ardor drew him from his mountain home—I, too, "longed to follow to the field some warlike lord;" and my honored father, himself a disciple of Jefferson, more propitious than young Norval's sire, pointed to that Senator, as a leader most fit for me to follow. From that time, in armor suited to my years, "with bended bow and quiver full of arrows, I hovered about the enemy, and marked the road he took." Nor did I lose sight of my chosen leader. My eye was fixed upon the white plume of "free trade" which waved so bravely from his "bonnet o' blue"—my ear lost no sound of his clarion voice, as it rang out from the summit of "Red Mountain," reverberating among the lesser hills of Hertford and Northampton, and ran along the valleys, even of the Meherrin and Chowan, arousing the slumbering genius of "State sovereignty." And my very heart leaped up with a joyous exultation, as I saw "monopoly" after "monopoly" go down before "the fateful steel" of his broad claymore, until not one "monster" of that hated clan was left. Such, sir, is a transcript of my faithful memory of those days—doubtless less vivid than the original impression. I thus followed the same leader until 1832, and through that memorable year. Then, by some mischance, I will not say how or to whom, I missed him. Here, perhaps, the curtain had as well be dropped, except to say that when I next was able to take a full and unobstructed view of his position and pursuit, the color of his plume was changed, and the black weeper of "*protection*" was in its place; the cry of "State sovereignty" had died upon his lips, and he murmured, not loud, but deep, Federal "*consolidation*," in its stead; and instead of striking, as of old, *against* "monopolies," I found, and still find him, upholding them with all his Bruce-like power. Here the curtain shall fall. I am, in all sincerity, grateful to the honorable Senator for much I learned from his precepts and example some twenty-odd years ago. I trust I do no injustice to his present position.

But to return to the tariff of 1828. That year witnessed the expulsion of the "monopolists" from Executive power; and then commenced the real struggle for the repeal of "the bill of abominations." It is needless to do more than allude to the fact of that struggle, or the crisis in the fate of the Union to which it led in 1832 and 1833. Those incidents are but too fresh and painful in the minds of all; and many yet survive, who are still unhealed of wounds received in the struggle which developed them. It is enough that the crisis was so imminent, that extremes met; and, as it were of necessity, joined hands in a "compromise," which, allowing ten years to equalize its burdens and its benefits, was solemnly agreed to be a sacred league and covenant that, upon the questions it adjusted, there should be no more strife among brethren forever. And for ten years, that covenant was kept; for during that period, the friends of "free trade" were in power; and they, as they have ever done, kept their faith. But, at the end of that period, by remarkable coincidence, the "monopolists" gained power, again. And, sad spectacle it was—sad for the country! in the very hour of their triumph, and as if to signalize it by a deed which might mark the age that witnessed its perpetration, with a stone so black that the memory of man should never efface its impression—in that hour, they broke that covenant, which had owed its existence almost to the death-throes of the Union—had been sealed, as it were, with the heart's blood of the nation, and been ratified by vows which can never be violated with impunity. But those vows were violated, as I have said; and, sure and swift, followed punishment in the track of the violation. The tariff act of 1842, returning to high protection, was erected upon the ruins of the compromise of 1833. Again was the country agitated; again were the Stuart's expelled; and again were the friends of "free trade" restored to power. Upon that, followed the tariff act of 1846; a return, in substance, to the compromise—a revenue tariff—of 1833; and once again, upon this question, the country was at rest. And so, upon that question, it has remained until this time; for, although the "monopolists" under a new name, under peculiar circumstances, and upon no distinct nor definite issues of public policy, gained access to Executive power, in 1848, and retain it now, they have not yet been bold enough to disregard the past, or venture upon that experiment directly, or in any palpable form, which has ever proved fatal to their predecessors of the same faith.

My object in making this incidental recurrence to the history and consequences of the tariffs, or protective legislation of this Government, has not been to revive unpleasant memories—nor to enter into any argument against it, further than to remind the Senate and the country how disturbing and injurious that legislation has been to the general interest of the country, sometimes even threatening the very existence of the Union itself; and all this, without conferring that benefit upon the particular interest it was designed to protect, which led to its adoption. For, after all, what has been the effect upon manufactures, of all this much-coveted protection? *Fluctuation*, FLUCTUATION—the greatest curse, a curse which no benefit, nor all benefits combined, can compensate—has been its unfailing and fatal attendant. As I said before, it stimulates the business for the time; and, thus encouraged, investments are extended, operations are enlarged, and expenses multiplied; and, as a consequence of this, the productions are excessively increased. And this, not in view of the real wants of the country, nor in accordance with the laws of demand and supply, which alone ever have given, or can give, stability and success to any legitimate or useful pursuit: but, growing out of mere enactments of arbitrary, special legislation, conceived in a spirit as narrow as the single interest it would subserve, it neither comprehends the relations which necessarily subsist between every other interest, and every pursuit, nor is competent to sustain the conflicts which, like "a comet shot madly from its sphere," it must unavoidably encounter in its eccentric course, among interests with which if left, undisturbed, to the general laws, it would be in perfect harmony. That this is so, I appeal to the manufacturers themselves, whether, in their workshops at home, or here by their enlightened Representatives in both Houses of Congress. If it be otherwise, what mean these jeremiads, and tales of terrible disaster, which crowd the columns of every newspaper, of factories closed, of operatives without employment, of fortunes ruined, of opulence reduced to beggary? Or, perhaps, more significant still, what mean those numerous memorials which besiege the doors, and pile the tables, and fill the committee-rooms, of Congress, session after session, for "protection! protection! more protection!" Sir, it is like a hot-bed crying for more fire, to sustain its unnatural plants, sickly from artificial nutrition, and weak from excessive growth, against the bracing atmosphere which gives life, and vigor, and healthy luxuriance to every other tree, and shrub, and fruit-bearing herb, which God intended for the proper use of man, and which always thrives best under the influence of his natural laws. Sir, you hear none of these complaints, and receive none of these memorials, from the farmers and planters of the country. And the cause of this is twofold: First, because, as I have said, their pursuits are left in the hands of those who best know how to conduct them, and thrive, as they progress, in the free and wholesome air of individual intelligence, enterprise, and exertion, and under the operation of their own general and salutary laws. And secondly, because of the more manly, and independent, and self-relying spirit those pursuits are calculated to foster and maintain.

And all this, Mr. President, brings me back almost to the starting-point of my argument, and resolves itself into the general principle with which I set out—that the Government should restrict itself to the exercise of its few, simple, well-defined functions, by means of general laws, of equal, uniform, and universal application; leaving, not *placing*, all men and all pursuits, upon the same relative and substantial footing, which nature gave them; and trusting individual pursuits to individual choice, and the results of their industry to be determined by the general laws of demand and supply.

Now, sir, if these general propositions be true—and I apprehend there are few members of the political party to which I belong, and which are in a decided majority in this Chamber, who will deny them—I say, if these be true, and more especially if, as I have undertaken to show, and as the same party has always maintained, they be applicable to the agricultural and manufacturing interests, why—*why*, I ask, are they not applicable—why shall they not be applied—to the *commercial* pursuits of our people?

Sir, it needs no industrious search after facts, and still less does it require a labored or ingenious argument, to answer this question. The facts are before us, and before the world. They are to be seen from the dome of this Capitol. They are to be seen on every river, and harbor, and "inland sea," of this vast continent of ours. They are asserted with a boldness which startles the world, under every sky, where float the stars and stripes from an American mast, and where every sea is cut by the swift keel of an American ship, whether that ship be wafted by the free winds of heaven, or propelled by the steam of American genius. The growth and vigor of our commercial marine, and especially the rich argosies of commerce which it wafts to and from our shores, and through every vein and artery of our land, are among the chief glories and boasts of the nation. And yet, they, sir, starting from nothing, have grown and flourished, as the commerce of no other people in the whole world has ever grown and flourished, since the Phœnicians first ventured in little boats from Aradus to Mount Carmel, to the hour when the last new clipper left her "ways" at Baltimore, to shame the naval architecture of the world. And all this growth and glory, without protection—without any help from the Government. All of it, sir, achieved by the genius and enterprise of individual people, left to the exercise of their own free thoughts, and to the untrammeled use of their own skillful hands. Go, sir, to Maine—I appeal to her Senators, now present—has she ever had, or does she now demand, protection for her one hundred and twenty-seven ships, her seventy-five brigs, her one hundred and fifteen schooners, all built in the single year 1850, making an aggregate of one hundred thousand tons for that year? Go to Maryland—I appeal, also, to her Senators—has she ever had, or does she now demand, protection for her one hundred and twenty-five clippers, built in 1850, which are the models for the world? Go, sir, to the West—to western Pennsylvania, to Ohio, to Kentucky, to Missouri—but no, sir, I will not go there. Their Senators are here, but I do not now appeal to them. I will not trust myself to do that *now*. If I did, I should speak too much, perhaps, from my heart, and consume the day—nay, I might consume a week upon that single theme. But this I will say, and say it now, for the West, that we have had no *protection*, and we ask none. We want nothing, and we ask nothing, but *justice* and *equality* in the operation of your laws. Neither of these, which are our guarantied rights under the Constitution, have we ever had. I may have more to say on one point in this connection, presently.

But to return, sir, to the protection of commerce. I deny—and I think the facts sustain me—that commerce, or navigation, as a legitimate, special interest, needs protection; and even if it did need such protection, I could never give it by special or exclusive laws, by which other interests, equally entitled to it, and equally important, shall inevitably be put at disadvantage, or be made to pay tribute to its advancement.

Mr. President, my strength has failed me. I was quite unwell when I began, and am unable to stand on my feet any longer. I hope, therefore, it will be agreeable to the Senate to postpone the subject till to-morrow, when, if able to be here, I will conclude what I have to say.

The postponement was agreed to.

MONDAY, *May* 17, 1852.

Mr. BORLAND resumed:

When, Mr. President, I was compelled, from illness, to suspend the remarks I was making upon this question, last Wednesday, the Senate was kind enough to postpone the subject; and, even next day, when I was yet too ill to be present, a further postponement was permitted, in courtesy to me. This is the first moment when I could resume my remarks. I tender my grateful acknowledgments for the courtesy extended to me; and now proceed with the discussion, from the point at which I was compelled to leave it.

I had then concluded my general views of the question before us, and of the principles involved in its discussion. I come now to the application of those principles to this particular amendment.

And this brings up some special examination of this Collins line of steamers. To what branch of the business of the country does this line belong? Which of the great interests, or industrial pursuits, does it represent? The answer I have given, and which I have undertaken to show is the true answer to these questions, is, that it comes under the head of commerce—that is, commerce and navigation combined, which are here inseparable, and may be treated under one head.

Then, sir, what is there peculiar to this line, which removes it beyond, or lifts it above, the rule we apply to other ships, or other commercial interests?

> "Upon what meat doth this our Cæsar feed,
> That he is grown so great?"

I anticipate the answer Mark Antony will give. Oh, sir, I know it—I have heard it—I have read it here, there, everywhere. And I might have seen, and perhaps enjoyed it too, "or a part thereof," had I but visited "the beautiful *Baltic*," when she came a-wooing here, some month or two ago—another *Venus*, from the froth of the sea, as she rose upon the vision of admiring thousands, and stood revealed in all the nude voluptuousness of her charms, without even the hands covering the chaste genius of *Praxiteles* has thrown before the Cnidian statue of the goddess,—leading in her train *Bacchus*, with his cups, to intoxicate the brain; and perhaps, too, the boy-god son of the zoned *Cyprian*, bearing, with arch and graceful impudence, his heart-compelling quiver. And we all know that *Orpheus* was there, as he certainly was here, with his negromantic lyre, strung to the modern "higher law," and played upon by steam, who successfully *moved* even this grave Senate to adjourn; and, as he sung, I almost fancied that we—

> ——"sat upon a promontory,
> And heard a mermaid, on a dolphin's back,
> Uttering such dulcet and harmonious breath,
> That the rude sea grew civil at her song;
> And certain '*stars* shot madly from their spheres,'
> To hear the sea-maid's music."

And I know not how many, or what other, profane gods and goddesses besides, were there, to mingle and minister at the institution of *Saturnalia* for this capital of the New World. But, sir, not possessing a soul so easily as others "moved by the concord of sweet sounds," nor yet, I trust, more fit than they "for treason, stratagem, and spoils," I was not led away, by the ears, on that occasion. It was I, as you may remember, who cried, "Get thee behind me, Satan!" And, thanks to the spirit of the sacred phrase, I was not led into that temptation.

Mr. President, the answer, however, which I have heard and read so much, has not satisfied me. It does not satisfy me yet; and I apprehend it never will or can, for the reason that I have not found it in accordance with the facts, nor consonant with the principles which govern my judgment, and determine my votes.

But, Mr. President, the history of this line, and the circumstances under which it comes before us, have suggested another answer which, while it is certainly clearer, and more comprehensible, is also more in accordance with what I understand the facts to be. And that, sir, is the vast amount of *capital* invested in this enterprise; consisting, as that capital does, nominally at least, of large sums of money—some $3,000,000, or more—and of a fund and a force of mental shrewdness, boldness, pertinacity, and want of delicacy, it has never before been my fortune to witness, and which it sometimes amazes me to contemplate. Such a capital is potent, beyond all my powers of computation. I doubt if my honorable friend from North Carolina, [Mr. BADGER,] armed with that *Dilworth's* arithmetic of his, and even my honorable friend from Kentucky, [Mr. UNDERWOOD,] with the talisman of his "square root," were to come to my assistance, whether even then, we could estimate the sum of that potency, or trace it out in all its ramifications.

But to be serious, sir, this much we have seen, and do know: the influence of this line has already full sway in the *Executive* counsels of this Government—it has already the monopoly of the newspaper press of this Metropolis; and, remorseless still, like some huge and hungry Boa Constrictor, it is fast winding its tortuous and fearful folds about the body and limbs of this Congress, until our strong ribs are giving way, and our very heart seems ready to be squeezed out, in the ghastly form of appropriations, which, if this pressure be not removed, will pour the life-blood of the National Treasury into the capacious and rapacious maws of bankers and speculators. Already, *hundreds of thousands* have thus been squeezed out and swallowed up. The cry is still for "*more!*" And now, *millions* upon *millions* are demanded! A few days will determine whether that demand shall be granted.

And, *apropos*, Mr. President, of the influence this line is bringing to bear upon us, and which I have called a "pressure:" A remark which fell the other day from the honorable Senator from Michigan, [Mr. CASS,] and which suggested this designation, struck me with great force. I will read it:

> "Sir, you know, and we all know, that *there is a great external pressure* in favor of all subjects of this kind; and *it should be guarded against and resisted with ceaseless vigilance*, or it will, in time, acquire an ascendency, *injurious to the best interests of the country.*"

Here, Mr. President, is the original of the idea—no, sir, I am wrong; not the *idea*, for my own observation had suggested that; but of the terms in which I have attempted to *express* the idea of the influences which are operating to squeeze this appropriation out of us. Sir, the Senator was right; he called things, as he usually does, by their right names, and gave us a fair and salutary warning, "that there is a great external pressure;" that "it should he guarded against and resisted;" "or it will prove injurious to the best interest of the country." I, myself, have felt this "pressure;" the Senator from Michigan [Mr. CASS] must have felt it, too, to have characterized it so well. I sincerely regret that we cannot have his *vote* to help us to comply with his *advice* to resist it.

And still, sir, holding to the Constrictor, I am reminded of the description which an Oriental traveler has given of one of these monsters he saw in the Island of Ceylon. It was fifty feet long, and strong in proportion; and, after long lying in wait, had just succeeded in capturing a large musk ox. I need not give the whole description, though it is interesting. At the close of it, however, he quaintly but graphically says:

> "As the folds tightened, and the broad chest of the noble but now suffering animal began to yield under the great external pressure, its bones were snapping with a noise as of so many pistol shots, and strange sounds were emitted from its laboring throat."

But, sir, to return to the question: what is there peculiar to this line, which should exempt it from the rule we apply to all other ships, and their associated commercial interests? To my mind, there is nothing which should do so. Inasmuch, however, as various reasons have been assigned why this should be done, I will briefly examine the main ones upon which reliance seems to be placed by the friends of the proposition.

First, then, the ships of this line are said to be

adapted to *war purposes.* I have already alluded to this, and expressed the opinion that, although the contract required it, and it was the only ground upon which a sufficient number of votes could be got for the original appropriation, yet it is a condition which has not been complied with. And this opinion is based upon what certainly are significant and, I think, conclusive facts and circumstances. I have said, and I repeat, that apart from every other circumstance in the case, the proposition of the Senator from North Carolina, [Mr. BADGER,] a leading friend of the measure, to turn this whole line over to the Post Office Department, was proof, to me, that it was no suitable nor proper part of our naval establishment; was, indeed, a virtual, as well as an actual abandonment, by those competent to judge, and authorized to speak, of the whole original ground of *war purposes.* And if this needed corroboration, that was surely furnished by that admission the Senator from Texas [Mr. RUSK] made, incidentally, to the Senator from Florida, [Mr. MALLORY,] that this line has "a seeming, and only a seeming connection" with the Navy, to which I have already alluded.

Mr. RUSK. All that I said was, that the expenses charged upon the books of the Treasury to this service, ought not to be charged either to the Post Office or to the Navy fund proper, and estimated as appropriations for either of those Departments. That was all that I said in relation to that point. But so far from admitting that these vessels were not suitable for war purposes, I stated at the time, if I remember aright, that they had been examined by a board of respectable naval officers, appointed for that purpose; that they had been pronounced suitable, and had been accepted by the Government.

Mr. BORLAND. I remember, very well, that the Senator said so. I am not speaking of his opinion. I am only stating the facts. When I made this allusion before, the Senator made a similar explanation to the one he has now given. He thought I gave an erroneous interpretation of his remarks. What he *did* say, may not have fairly represented what he *meant;* but I apprehend, as his remark was reported in the papers, it would be understood by the country precisely as I interpreted it. The other day, when I made the allusion, I did not have before me the Senator's remarks. I have since examined them, in print, and now have them before me.

In opposition to the amendment offered by the Senator from Florida, [Mr. MALLORY,] and appealing to him, he said:

"Is he willing to separate the Navy from *a seeming, and only a seeming connection with this line,* by throwing it upon those who pay postage upon letters, throughout the country?"

I think my interpretation of this was the only one it would naturally bear. And I think, further, it derives additional propriety, if needed, from the suggestion, evidently made, in his opinion then expressed, that the whole policy of making the Post Office Department dependent upon its own revenues was wrong; and that as the payment of this mail service directly from the Treasury was, *pro tanto,* a correction of that wrong, he was for continuing to make it there. Nowhere, in that connection, did he even intimate that this service (mark, it is *mail service*) should be paid for out of the general Treasury, upon the ground that the line which performed it was a part of the Navy. On the contrary, in special reference to this very point, he declared the connection between this line and the Navy to be "seeming, and only seeming." I could draw no other inference than I did. But the Senator says now, it is his opinion that these steamers *are* suitable for "war purposes," and may, in time of need, be made useful as such. For the Senator's opinion I have great respect, as I have entire confidence in his candor. He must excuse me, however, if I cannot adopt his opinion, when I do not find it sustained by what my mind can recognize as facts; and more especially, when I do find it opposed by an incidental argument of his own, which strikes me as of great force and significance. But, besides this general reason, there are some special reasons for denying that these ships are adapted to "war purposes."

We have it from reliable authority, and it was so stated here by the Senator from Florida, [Mr. MALLORY,] who is familiar with such things, and it has not been denied, that these ships are built of unsuitable materials for war service; that their outer walls are made of "*pine* plank;" whereas, those of all vessels of war are made of *oak;* and that their "timbers and frames" are a "mixture of live-oak, locust, and pine;" whereas the "timbers and frames" of all vessels of war are made of live-oak. Why was this? Will any one undertake to say that live-oak, and all other kinds of wood used in naval architecture, and that, too, in abundance, and of the best quality, cannot be had at any and all of our yards? Why, then, was this light, unusual, and unsuitable material made use of in the construction of these ships? Sir, but one answer can be given—certainly, in view of the facts, but one should be received—and that is, they were never intended for "war purposes," and therefore were not built of materials suited to those purposes.

Again: it has been objected, and upon what I must receive as good authority—certainly as respectable for character and competency, as any which has been adduced on the other side, and superior in number of witnesses, and in the directness, point, and force of their statements—that, besides their defective material, the *structure* of these ships unfits them for "war purposes," or for easy conversion to such purposes.

Of the persons who have been called in to sustain the character of these ships for convertibility into war steamers, I find Commodore Perry, Captain Skiddy, and Mr. Francis Grice, a naval constructor, the main, if not the only ones relied upon. This, I confess, has struck me with some surprise, and is, at any rate, a very significant circumstance. I can well understand how it is that the testimony of any great number of naval officers has not been given or presented here *against* the war character of these ships. Being officers of the Government which they find engaged in an enterprise of seeming great importance, and under the orders of an Administration that they know to be favorable to that enterprise, what more natural, if not actually becoming, than for them to remain silent at least, and abstain from what might be regarded by their superiors, as unwarranted and officious? And I can appreciate, also, the motive, as well as official delicacy, which would restrain them from coming forward unasked with their opinions, especially if those opinions were unfavorable to the views of the Administration, or to any private interests.

But, sir, *some* have been asked—how many I do not know, and a *few* have given their opinions. Of those, as I have said, the three whose names I have mentioned, seem to be all who have spoken favorably—certainly all who have been relied upon as authority to sustain the naval character of these ships. I repeat, sir, that, to my mind, this is both surprising and significant—surprising that so small a foundation has been supplied for so large a superstructure as has been attempted to build upon it; significant of the general condemnation which the officers of our Navy have given to this new system.

And of these three witnesses who have been brought forward for these ships, Commodore Perry is the first in rank, and perhaps the first in authority. And even he is summoned by both the prosecution and defense. The Senator from Texas, [Mr. RUSK,] as now the leading advocate of this line, quotes him to prove that these ships have been properly constructed, and may, at no great additional cost, be adapted to "war purposes." But, then, he is also quoted by the Senator from Virginia, [Mr. HUNTER,] to show that the witness's own statement is exceedingly indefinite and unsatisfactory. It is true he does say, as quoted by the Senator from Texas, in speaking of the Baltic, (and I take her as the best, and this as the summary of the best he has said of her:)

"Although not in accordance with every particular stipulation of the contract, as has already been made known to the Department, by the superintendent in charge, she is constructed of suitable dimensions, build, and finish, to conform with the contract for carrying the mails on her destined route, and with the preparations and additions of suitable war appointments, she could be easily converted into a war steamer of the first class."—*November* 2, 1850.

February 18, 1852, he says:

"According to my calculation, the cost of the conversion of either of the before-mentioned vessels, exclusive of armaments, repair of machinery, and ordinary repair, would not, or certainly *ought* not, exceed, for steamers of the first class, $20,000, and for those of the second class, $15,000; and it could be readily done for this at any of our navy-yards, provided that *useless* alterations were not made. * * *

"The armaments of the respective vessels would, of course, be a separate cost; and to arrange the guns on the upper deck, it would only be required to close up three or four of the hatches or sky-lights; to strengthen the deck by additional beams and stanchions; to cut ports, and construct the pivot and other carriages; probably it might be desirable to shift the capstan and cables."

But here, again, as quoted on the other side by the Senator from Virginia, he says:

"The mail steamers of the contracts of Howland & Aspinwall, of George Law, and of E. K. Collins, can be easily converted into war steamers for temporary service, in cases of particular emergency. These vessels, with little strengthening of the decks, can be made to carry each a few guns of heavy caliber, and may be rendered useful to convoy, in the transportation of troops, carrying dispatches, conveying public functionaries, &c., &c.; but their service could only be contingent, and, as before remarked, *temporary*.

"The cost of converting them to war purposes would be large, and in no respect would they be as economical, or in any way equal to vessels built expressly for Government service; nor should they, in my opinion, interfere in the least with the organization and gradual increase of an efficient and permanent steam navy. The use of steamships in our future naval operations must inevitably change in a great degree the art of naval war. Indeed no one can imagine what changes will be effected, as well upon the ocean as upon the land, by means of the new agencies which have been more practically developed within the last quarter of a century."—*April* 9, 1850.

Extracts from a letter to the Secretary of the Navy, from Commodore M. C. Perry, of 18th of February, 1852:

"It will be well, however, to premise that, under no circumstances, and at whatever cost, can a steam-vessel, built expressly for the transportation of freight or passengers, be made, in any manner, equal in convenience and efficiency to a vessel originally intended for war purposes, even assuming that the materials of which the respective vessels are constructed are in all respects equal. And for the obvious reason, that in the construction of a vessel of war, from the laying of the keel, every part of the vessel is, in the progress of completion, made subservient to the accommodation and arrangement of the armament, the safe-keeping of the munitions, provisions, water, &c., and the berthing of the several classes of officers, and the crew; while in mail or packet steamers—in this country—no preparations are made for any armament, the ingenuity of the builder being alone taxed to render them extravagantly showy and best adapted for the accommodation of numerous passengers and the stowage of freight."

* * * * * * *

"*Question first.* 'Whether the steamships employed in 'the transportation of the United States mail, under contract with the Navy Department, or any other steamships 'employed in the transportation of our foreign mails, are, 'in all respects, suitable for immediate conversion into 'steamers for war purposes, capable of carrying the armament or battery appropriate to the class specified in the 'contract?'

"In answer to the foregoing [first] question, I am of opinion that they are '*not* in all respects suitable.'"

* * * * * * *

"It should be taken into view that those mail steamers, if called into service as war vessels, would be considered as forming an auxiliary force to the regularly-constructed ships, and hence the impolicy of expending much money on them. The requisites of sound hulls and powerful engines, with efficient armaments, should alone be considered, leaving superfluous ornament out of the question."

So much for Commodore Perry as a witness in this case. I make no question of his candor in either of the somewhat conflicting statements he has here made. I am only dealing with his statements as I find them. It will be observed that his last statements, as here quoted on each side, are of the same date, February 18, 1852. Let those reconcile their discrepancy who can. If it may be said to preponderate on either side, I think it is against these ships—certainly against the system under which they were contracted for. But, upon the whole, I think he has so far ridden on "both sides of the sapling" at the same time, that his testimony may well be dispensed with altogether. And I feel very sure that, in a court of justice where the "rights of person or of property" were to be decided between individuals, although a very technical judge might admit his statements to sustain some "special plea" upon that very lucid and elastic phrase "war purposes;" yet any intelligent and fair-minded jury, who desired to ascertain the real merits of the case, would certainly "set him aside." But, I confess, I have some curiosity to see an experiment tried upon the Commodore himself, and that is, to offer him this Collins line of steamers for his East India squadron, with which he is going out as a missionary to the isolated Japanese, to whom, it seems, for some mysterious purpose, supposed to be *political*, our present Federal Executive deems it salutary to administer a little *American opium*, or something stronger, from the muzzles of certain heavy guns upon "land carriages." I apprehend the experienced Commodore would hardly risk them for even such "war purposes" as that. If he did, I should regard him as a fit companion for those famous "three wise men of Gotham, who went to sea in a bowl."

I observe, here, another thing that seems significant. It is the peculiar character of the certificates which *Mr. John Lenthall* (whom I take to be a naval constructor) appends to the Commodore's several reports in favor of the several ships of this line.

Mr. STOCKTON, (in his seat.) He is among the ablest and most experienced of our naval constructors.

Mr. BORLAND. I have no doubt of it. Then, *Mr. Lenthall* says:

"I concur in this report, as to her being a *mail* steamer of the first class."

And he says no more. But that is a point that no one questions. "Mail steamers of the first class" we admit them to be. It is their being suitable for "war purposes," that we question and deny. This gentleman seems cautious and prudent in his certificate, and is, no doubt, reliable. I shall have occasion to use his testimony upon another point in this connection, presently.

Next comes Captain Skiddy, upon whom the honorable Senator from Texas [Mr. RUSK] lays great stress. I find his statements coincide, substantially, with those of Commodore Perry, in favor of these particular ships; with this advantage for them, that he does not contradict himself.

Mr. Francis Grice, a naval constructor, is the third authority upon whom the advocates of these ships rest their claims to be suitable for "war purposes." Well, he is a good witness for the parties who have introduced him, to the extent of his competency and credibility; for he certifies to all they desire—to rather more, I apprehend, than the Senator from North Carolina [Mr. BADGER] believes to be true. He was first introduced by the Senator from New Jersey, [Mr. MILLER,] and afterwards by the Senator from North Carolina. He is clearly *in*, for all sorts of "war purposes."

I now come to the witnesses on the other side. It will be remembered that Commodore Perry has been "set aside," or stands neutral as to the ships; and is against the system.

First, then, on this side, I introduce an extract from the report of Commodore Charles William Skinner, to the Secretary of the Navy:

"7. What is the best instrument for propelling commercial ocean steamers, the paddle-wheel or submerged screw? and do these instruments require different models for the hull?

"*Answer.* The paddle-wheel is generally considered the best instrument of propulsion where speed is required; but for the purposes of war the screw would be preferable, and they do require different models.

"8. Do you consider commercial ocean steamers, as now built, convertible at once into war steamers, and capable of efficiently performing war service?

"*Answer.* They cannot be converted into war steamers without great expense, and then they would be inferior to those designed solely for that purpose."

This, I think, will do for a set-off to Captain Skiddy.

Second, comes Mr. Haswell, Chief Engineer of our Navy. His testimony, I apprehend, will stand a comparison with that of Mr. Grice. It is this:

"With a large majority of the commercial ocean steamers now built, the proportions, capacities, and construction of their hulls, and the design and arrangement of their engines and boilers, are such as to render them incapable of efficient and economical war service, without incurring an expenditure in alterations and a loss of time that would not, except in cases of national emergency, be at all repaired by the ultimate durability of the hulls of the vessels in their ready transfer to, or in their economical performance of active service."

* * * * "They are so deficient in stability, *without the spars and armament of a naval steamer*, that it is necessary to depress them beyond their intended limits, in order to effect their passages with the probability of security."

* * * * * "The steamers of Mr. Collins's line, now in progress of construction, will cost $550,000 each. Yet the boilers of these vessels, and all the other mail steamers, are of iron, their hulls are not constructed of live-oak, and the vessels are without the spars, rigging, armament and equipment of naval steamers." * *

"The first mail steamers have proved inadequate to their service, from the insufficiency of their construction; and after but two and a half years' service, and at a cost of repairs and alterations exceeding their first cost, they are now incapable of any useful naval purpose; they, therefore, an ignorance of their worthlessness existing, are estimated in our means of naval defenses; and when required for such purpose, the dependence would prove as disastrous to our national interests as their construction has been to our professional reputation as constructors and engineers."

Upon the points touched upon so far, I think the testimony overwhelming and conclusive, to prove that these ships are not suitable for "war purposes."

In respect to the means and mode of propelling ocean steamers, and especially as to the mode adopted in these ships, there is difference of opinion. But in reference to that mode, as connected with "war purposes," the weight of testimony is still more against them, if that be possible, than upon the other points I have already examined.

I allude particularly here to the difference between the "side wheels, or paddles," and the "screw," usually called the "propeller." All these ships of the Collins line are "*paddle-wheels.*"

I do not know that I can better express my own opinion upon this point than by quoting a short paragraph from the speech of the honorable Senator from Ohio, [Mr. WADE,] delivered here last Monday. He said:

"I know nothing of war or of naval operations, nor do I profess to know anything about them; but any man of the least common sense, at the very first glance at these steamers, would perceive that they were not designed for the purposes of war. Nor are they compatible with it at all. *Why, one cannon-ball, raking the paddle-wheels—which form a most palpable mark—of one of those steamers, would cripple her as effectually as a man could cripple a goose on the wing.* Talk about their utility as vessels of war! I know they would not be of the slightest use."

Nor, sir, does the Senator from Ohio stand alone in this opinion; for, without counting myself, there is high and decisive authority for giving the "screw" the preference over the "paddles," particularly for "war purposes," and indeed for all purposes of ocean navigation, especially on long voyages. But, in view of the obvious nature of the case itself, it seems to me that but little authority is needed beyond ordinary powers of observation, and a fair allowance of common sense, to enable and compel any man to determine for himself that this must be so. When we consider that the paddle-wheels of a steamer are a "most palpable mark," as expressed by the Senator from Ohio—a mark that could hardly be missed by an enemy's shot; and further, that upon those wheels depend the whole means the ship possesses to make her way through the water, the conclusion seems to me equally palpable with the wheels, that the whole fabric is most exposed in its most vital part, and is constantly liable to be crippled and knocked up by a single shot, or at most, by a couple of shots, from an enemy's gun. Break the wheels of the largest and best appointed steamer which floats upon the Atlantic—"the beautiful Baltic," if you please, even best adapted to "war purposes," and such an accident might easily happen from a single cannon shot—and she would, indeed, lie like "a crippled goose" upon the waters, rolling, helpless in the trough of the sea. And I apprehend that he who had "gone down to the sea" in her, would feel very much like a crippled goose, also, as he lay at the mercy of the enemy's fire, unable to attack, unable to escape!

On the contrary, the "screw-propellers" are perfectly safe in this respect. All their machinery is below the "water line," and the screw itself is deeply submerged below the stern of the ship; thus not only securing all the motive power against the reach of danger, but leaving the deck flush, and the broadsides of the ship to be filled with guns, as in the regular man-of-war; and permitting the hull to be fashioned after such a model as shall best give strength and facility of motion.

And here I had as well add, that in the side-wheel ships, it is not alone the "paddles" that are exposed, but the engine itself, the whole machinery of motion, is *above* the water. This, it is true, is mainly covered by the upper decks, a very frail covering at best, while the vessel remains, as she was built, a *merchant* ship or *mail* steamer. But everybody concurs in the statement, and we all know the fact, that the first step towards converting such a ship into a vessel-of-war, must be to remove those upper decks; and although such protection as they afforded was almost nominal, yet their removal certainly, completely, and at once, exposes all the machinery, as well as the paddles, to every kind of missile from an enemy. And there is no remedy for the evils of this exposure. The position of the machinery cannot be shifted. When the ship was built, every part and appurtenance designed to be permanent, was placed in its appropriate position, and accurately adjusted to every other portion, so as to secure due concert of action among the several parts, and the greatest power and facility of motion, as a whole. If any of the material conditions of this arrangement be changed, the equilibrium will be disturbed and the harmony of parts destroyed. The upper decks are originally intended to be removed, upon occasion, and are constructed accordingly. When removed, this beautiful bird of the sea, to which they had before given some pretense of shelter and protection, must go forth entirely naked and exposed, alike in her wings and her vitals, or she cannot go forth at all.

But I said there was good authority for these opinions—and I am not aware of any against them. And here I will introduce Mr. Lenthall again.

Extracts from Mr. John Lenthall's letter to Commodore C. W. Skinner, dated 18th of February, 1852:

"I would, in the first place, state, that there is some doubt whether a side-wheel steamer can be made into a war steamer of the first class.

"The machinery of such a steamer should be placed below the level of common dangers from shot; and to enable her to become a cruiser requires that she should be a perfect sailing vessel in all respects—not only in the power of the sail, but also in its position. The fullness of the extremities should be such that the motions of pitching and ascending may be within moderate limits, and they should be able to support the heavy guns at their extremities, which are deemed essential to their armament. It is desirable that they should be fast vessels, but they must be capable of using as well as carrying their armament; and as no other quality can compensate for a deficiency in this, it becomes a primary consideration."

* * * * * * * "The words 'suitable for immediate conversion into steamers for war purposes,' I understand to mean the state in which an actual ship of war would be if temporarily employed in carrying the mail or passengers.

"From the superficial examinations I had the opportunity of making, these ships appeared in about the same degree of readiness for immediate conversion into steamers for war purposes as merchant ships, according to their size and speed, are into frigates or other classes of ships of war possessing the advantages common to large vessels of a capacity permitting, if required, the additional materials necessary, and the armament and equipments required to be placed on board to make them war vessels."

Then, here is English authority upon the same subject, and from a source entitled to the highest respect:

Extracts from the "Minutes of Evidence taken before the Select Committee on Steam Navy," ordered by the British House of Commons in 1849.

At page 73 of the printed report, is the testimony of Captain W. H. Henderson, R. N., C. B., as follows:

"741. Do you think that vessels of that packet class, taking a superior class of vessels, might be made useful in the case of war, for channel purposes and protecting our coast, and for looking out? Very useful.

"742. But not to supersede men-of-war? No; I consider that they are a different kind of vessel; they are made for working against the head winds of the Atlantic, and they are under rigged, and are not intended for sailing."

At page 81, same report, is the testimony of Captain H. D. Chads, R. N., as follows:

"892. Do you think that they would supersede the use of steamships built expressly as ships-of-war? I should apprehend that we should make a sad mistake if we attempted to do away with our own. I think that under no circumstances could you apply them as men-of-war, strictly in the meaning of the term 'men-of-war.'

"893. You do not conceive that they are so well adapted for fighting purposes, and for keeping company with fleets, as ships that are built for the Royal Navy? I apprehend that they would be always required to be under steam, to keep company with our fleet; I do not think, from their rig, that they have sufficient canvas to enable them to keep way with our vessels without steaming; that they would be constantly under a certain portion of steam, consequently their coals would be soon exhausted."

At page 89, of same report, is the testimony of Rear-Admiral Sir Charles Napier, K. C. B., as follows:

"1015. Would you confine the use of those vessels to the channel, or would you make use of them by sending them abroad into our Colonies? I do not think they would be fit to go abroad with that fitting, which I think they ought to have at all times, because it is too late to begin to fit when the enemy is on your shores. I do not think they would be fit to go abroad, because they would be too small, and as the greater number of large ones would be abroad at the time, you would not be able to get hold of them."

From similar sources the honorable Senator from Virginia [Mr. HUNTER] makes the following brief, but pregnant summary:

"I omitted the testimony of Lieutenant Roberts, of the English navy, in 1848. He was asked whether the American steamers could carry guns? He said, no better than their own, and not quite so well as their own merchant steamers. I say, that these facts prove undoubtedly, that, according to the opinions of all, or almost all, the professional men of eminence, both in the British Navy and in ours—and my friend from Florida [Mr. MALLORY] tells me that such also is the practice and opinion in the French Navy—it is considered that no other steamer is fit for purposes of war except the screw-propeller."

And then, the same Senator condenses his opinion so forcibly and clearly, and sustains it so conclusively in another short paragraph, that I must be permitted to substitute his words for my own:

"I am authorized in saying, from all that I can see, and from all that I can learn, that it is now an admitted fact amongst professional men, that steamers with the paddle-wheel cannot be made efficient war-steamers—that the screw-propeller is the only mode of making a war-steamer which can be efficient. That is distinctly proved as the opinion of those English officers who were examined at the time to which I have referred. I have recently read a book of great interest, written by Captain Halstead, of the British Navy, in 1850, in which he demonstrates that fact. The screw-steamer is superior for these reasons: 1. She can carry a whole broadside, which a paddle-wheel steamer cannot carry. 2. Her machinery can be effectually protected from shot—and I am told that it was but last year, or the year before, that a British paddle-wheel steamer was disabled by a single shot fired from a slaver off the coast of Africa. 3. She can go to sea with a much less supply of coal, for she uses steam only as an auxiliary power to sails. She is capable of being built upon the finest models for strength and speed, which cannot be done with the side-paddle, because the necessity of carrying the armament fore and aft impairs the force of the ship."

I must here say, that I am not indebted to my own research for most of the facts and authorities which I have cited and relied upon. I have already said to the Senate that I have drawn largely, as I rely with confidence, in this respect, upon my honorable friend from Virginia, [Mr. HUNTER.] I have had his kind permission to do so, and avail myself of the privilege to take from one of his late speeches the following extracts:

"Extract from note accompanying the letter from Commodore Perry, of 18th February, 1852, from which the above extracts were taken:

"The deterioration of ocean mail steamers growing out 'of wear and tear and gradual decay, notwithstanding every 'possible repair, may be estimated at five per cent. per an-'num for live-oak ships—perhaps a trifle less."

"I could go further, and produce you the same sort of testimony from other sources; but that is enough. I know the friends of the amendment rely upon a letter which Commodore Perry wrote, and which, I suspect, is to be interpreted into an opinion that the ships might suit for temporary purposes—for transportation, and kindred services. I looked into the proceedings of the special committee to which I have referred, raised in the British Parliament, in 1848, upon the subject of steamships, and I found there the same opinion expressed by Captain Henry D. Chads, and by Captain Henderson, and by Admiral Napier, all of the Royal Navy. They said that their merchant steamers could not supersede the war steamers, and were not equal to them for war purposes. They all said that such steamers were not fit to send abroad, and would burn out all their coal before they could get abroad. But they said—what is true in their country—that they might be eminently serviceable for purposes of defense in time of an invasion—to defend the Channel in case their country should be invaded. It is evident that this examination was made under great apprehensions of a French invasion, for their inquiries seemed to be directed to that contingency. Upon being questioned, in order to ascertain whether they could make war steamers out of those ships, Captain Chads said, that if they were strengthened, fore and aft, so as to make them capable of carrying guns, they would lose the quality of superior speed; and he intimated that a British war steamer was not much more valuable for the quality of superior speed, if she was not able to fight anything of her cost and size. Of what advantage was that to her, but to run away?—and was that a quality which was valued in a British steamer? Sir, if that is a quality which is not to be valued in a British steamer, I would ask whether it should be highly valued in an American steamship of war?

"Now, if you will look to the testimony of Commodore Perry, you will find that he had some ideas of the same sort, for he italicizes the words "*for temporary purposes.*" And why for temporary purposes? You could not use them long. They would soon burn out their coal and use up their fuel. They could not carry guns enough for any extensive service."

"I find, too, that in the examination, in England, in 1848, Lord Auckland says the English are using the screw-propeller* to a large extent, as an auxiliary power in the merchant service; and Mr. Ward said that they had answered perfectly, in the Holland trade, when they had been tried. He was asked in 1848: 'Are you aware whether it has become common in the merchant service to use the screw-propeller?' He answered:

"'It is extending in the merchant service, and has pro-'duced some very curious results. The experiments had 'been particularly successful in the case of those small 'schooners which are built for the trade with Holland, and 'then they seem to have succeeded completely. They have 'engines which occupy only one seventh of the vessel, 'while the engines of the Blenheim occupy nearly one third. 'And they attain very considerable speed, eight knots, eight 'and a half knots, and nine knots. The screw is never 'raised. The apertures are all immersed, and the voyage 'of two hundred and sixty miles, upon a long series of ex-'periments, averages about thirty-six hours.'

"I was shown, this morning, a letter just received from Boston, from a gentleman of high authority and great experience in such matters, who says:

"'My opinion is so strongly in favor of propelling with 'strong auxiliary steam, that I believe if two steamers were 'to be sent on a survey, or a naval cruise of any kind, the 'paddle starting to-day, and the propeller being laid down a 'month hence, at the end of eighteen months the latter would 'be ahead in her work, at a cost fifty per cent. less! In 'short, the paddle must be constantly near the coal-yard 'and the machine-shop, while the other would be inde-'pendent of both.'

"Indeed, he says much to justify the opinion, that the screw-propeller, as an auxiliary, is destined to make a revolution in the merchant service. It is a fact of which I have no sort of doubt. I was told, on Monday, at the Navy Department, that they had made a comparison of the log of the '*San Jacinto*,' before her machinery broke down, with the log of the '*Saranac*;' the '*San Jacinto*' being a propeller, and the '*Saranac*' a side-wheel steamer. The '*Saranac*' beat the '*San Jacinto*' less than three per cent. in point of speed, while the superiority, in every other respect, was with the '*San Jacinto*.'"

"So that if we are to expend the money which ought to be expended in the gradual increase of the Navy in thus keeping up side-wheel merchant steamers, we will not only expend it in a service to which it will not be ultimately useful, but we take away a fund which is necessary, in order to increase the Navy in a mode which will be useful to it, and which will enable us to exercise our officers. Why, what is our policy in relation to the Navy? We seek to maintain just such a Navy, and no more, as will preserve the police of the seas, so far as it is incumbent on us to maintain that police. We also keep up a skeleton arrangement, capable of extension and expansion in time of war. To make that skeleton arrangement efficient, it is indispensable that we should have all possible means of exercising and training our young officers. How can we do it, if we expend the money on steamers to be commanded by merchant captains? And that is the case, I understand, with these Collins steamers. Ought we not to expend the money which we can devote to such services upon war steamers of proper models, and with proper machinery, so that our officers may command them, and be exercised in a steamer with all her appointments, and complete as to machinery, sails, and battery?"

The Secretary of the Navy, Mr. Graham himself, who seems to be in some sort relied upon by its friends in support of this line, is compelled, evidently with reluctance, to admit, from the discussions and testimony of competent naval officers, "that *vessels of this description cannot be relied on to supersede those modelled and built only for purposes of war.*" The highest merit he claims for them is that, while "*a limited number of them may be employed in time of peace in the transportation of the mail,*" they might also be useful upon "*the breaking out of war,*" as "*transports for troops and*

* "Extracts from a work entitled 'The Screw-fleet of the Navy,' by Captain E. P. Halstead, of the English Navy. He commends the adoption of screw-ships in the Brazil mail service, for the following reasons: At page 87—

"'Because it is a principle which is capable of reducing 'public expenditure, at the same time that it improves gen-'eral commerce. Because it takes less out of the public 'purse, and puts more into private ones, while paddle pro-'pulsion draws very largely upon both; for, instead of car-'rying goods, the paddle is compelled to carry coals only, 'and then it calls upon all of us to pay for the expense of 'burning them.'

"And again, he says, at page 89:

"'I am not in error when I state that the practical differ-'ence between paddle propulsion and screw propulsion, 'that is to say, between large ships carrying large cargoes 'of coal and small cargoes of goods, amounts to this, viz: 'That the auxiliaries are able to make a profitable return 'upon freights which are twenty-two per cent. lower than 'those demanded by the full powered steamer.'"

munitions of war;" but he looks to using them in no higher naval capacity than in the way mentioned, and as a sort of occasional "*privateers or guerrillas of the ocean;*" but only then "*fitted with such armaments as could be readily put on board, even in their present condition.*" This is his own language, in his report of March 8, 1852, in which he was evidently endeavoring to say all in their favor which conscience would permit. Under these circumstances, he not only does not pretend that these ships can be substituted for our vessels of war, but he expressly says they "*cannot be relied on*" for any such purpose. Mark, sir, this is said by the Secretary, in an official report, designed as the basis of Congressional action, and from the best professional advice which his command of the whole Navy could enable him to procure.

Now, what is the natural and unavoidable inference from all this? A Senator here and there may rise in his place, and tell me that *he believes* "these ships are as good for war purposes as any ships in the Navy." But, while I admit the honesty of that belief, and highly respect the general information and intelligence of those who entertain it, yet, to receive that for *proof* which shall *disprove* so much that is based on established *facts* and sustained by reason, is rather too large a pill for my credulity and complaisance, combined, to swallow at a single dose. Opinion and belief will not do for this occasion. *Proof* is required—it is indispensable. If it existed, the Secretary of the Navy, together with this very astute company, would certainly have it here before us. But it is not here; and though called for time and again, it is not forthcoming. I can infer only *that it does not exist.*

Surely I have said enough upon this problem of "war purposes," especially in reference to the Collins line of "paddle-wheels." I consider the problem solved. It certainly is to my own conviction. For the reasons I have adduced, and many others which might be brought forward, and which, I think, make proof, both circumstantial and positive, complete against them, I conclude that the ships of this line are not, in the true and proper sense, suitable for war purposes, and that, to answer such purposes to any really important or useful extent, can never be made so. The Senator from North Carolina was right, therefore, when he openly abandoned the ground that they were so, and proposed directly to turn them over to the Post Office Department. And the remark of the Senator from Texas was also true, whether he intended to be so understood or not, that the connection of this line with the Navy was "*seeming*, and *only* seeming."

Upon this ground, then, of "war purposes," this enterprise, however meritorious in other respects, is a failure, and must be abandoned. It is not exempt from the operation of the same rule, therefore, which, in our ordinary legislation, we apply to other navigating and commercial interests; and, therefore, it has no just claim to this allowance out of the Treasury.

And here, Mr. President, I think it not improper to notice what has seemed to me a somewhat extraordinary feature in the discussion of this question. Intimations have been thrown out by the friends of this measure, that Collins & Co. are very ill-used individuals—suffering patriots, and threatened victims, as it were, in their country's cause! Well, sir, such an attitude, for them, contrasts somewhat strongly in appearance, it is true, with the high pretensions under which they got the Government and themselves into the present difficulty. Yet is not so unnatural a transition after all; for mendicity and self-abasement form no unusual sequel to high pretensions, and magnificent display. It is intimated that there is a disposition, somewhere, to disregard the good faith of the Government in this case, and ruin Collins & Co. by a violation of their contract. Now, sir, it is as well that we should understand one another, and that the country, and Mr. Collins too, should understand us all, upon this point. Where, I ask, has any disposition been manifested, anywhere in Congress, to violate this contract, or to make its conditions even hard, upon Collins & Co.? I deny any such wish or intention, for myself, and for those with whom I am acting. Nor, sir, has any such wish or intention been evinced on any occasion, or in any respect whatever. The suggestion, that there has been any such thing in existence, is as unfounded in truth, as the claims of this company, to further favor at the hands of Congress, are unfounded in merit. This last, I think, has been pretty clearly shown already; and will, I further think, be placed beyond dispute, before I have done with it.

"The contract!" Well, sir, what of the contract? Gentlemen seem to forget its terms and conditions, as well as the circumstances under which it was entered into, and the manner of its prosecution. To prevent misapprehension, it is well we should recur to them. I have nothing particular to say of the beginning of this affair, when it was originally begged and bored through Congress. That was before my day here, and comes down to me as a part of the unwritten history of those times, from those who were here, and observers of what took place. But I am sure it has not been exaggerated to me, from my own observation since I came—especially in the advance of money for building these ships, and the extension of the time for completing them—and still more vividly in view of what has been going on all this session, and is now at work. I allude to that "great external pressure," which the honorable Senator from Michigan [Mr. CASS] reminded us of the other day, and which I have already likened to a huge snake, involving and compressing us in its powerful folds. But these considerations, much as they disgusted me before, and humiliate me now, do not affect my opinion of the contract itself, nor will they influence my course in regard to it. So far as it *is* a contract, I will observe its terms and conditions, myself, as fully and as firmly as any man who voted for it. And sir, I will go a step further, which some of those who have voted for it do not seem disposed to go—and that is, I will make the other parties observe it too. But further than that, on either side, I will not go.

I ask, again, what are the terms and conditions of this much-vaunted contract? Here are the facts: In November, 1847, Collins & Co., under the act of March 3d of that year, contracted to build, and have ready for service, *five* ships of a specified character, *four* of them at the expiration of eighteen months, and the *fifth* "as early as may be practicable thereafter;" and for the service of these ships, in carrying the United States mails across the Atlantic, the United States to pay them $385,000 a year, in quarterly payments, to begin after the service had commenced. This is the first contract. It binds both parties to do certain things.

The obligation is reciprocal. It is binding equally upon the company and the United States. And, bear in mind, sir, it was a contract, in all its terms and conditions, into which Collins & Co. actually begged, and bored, and teased the Congress, upon the earnest and reiterated assurance, that they could and would execute it promptly and faithfully. Well, what was the result? Why, sir, before half the time had expired, at the end of which they were to have four of these ships ready for service, (under this much-coveted contract of their own proposing,) this very sagacious company discovered that they had not the ability to execute their contract at all. So here they come back upon Congress, representing that unless we extended them some relief and assistance, the whole scheme must fall through and end in smoke. Then, to carry out this addition to their scheme, there commenced another series of begging and boring. I speak of this from my own observation, and it is familiarly known to the Senate. The result of this was a provision in the naval appropriation bill, of August 3, 1848, authorizing the Secretary of the Navy to advance to Collins & Co. $25,000 a month for each of their ships, to enable them to build them; that is, $100,000 a month for the four ships until they should be completed and ready for service. This was consummated under a supplemental contract, dated February 6, 1849. With this concession, which was all they pretended to ask for then, and far more than they had asked for in the beginning, this company expressed themselves satisfied, and gave renewed assurances of a speedy and faithful performance of their contract. But, again, what was the result? Why, sir, a month had not elapsed, perhaps not a day, before they discovered again that they were unable to fulfill their contract, and we had them upon us again, even more clamorous than before; thus proving, it would seem, that concessions of advantage to the speculator, like blood upon the tongue of a wolf, instead of appeasing, but serves to make his appetite ravenous for more. And so actively did they work, and sturdily beg, that from the 6th of February to the 3d of March, some twenty-five days, they got a provision in the naval appropriation bill, of the latter date, allowing them an extension of time to June 1, 1850, in which to finish their ships and begin their service; in the mean time, the advance of $100,000 a month to them to continue.

This is a true history of the transactions, under that famous contract, up to the beginning of this session of Congress; when it had reached its third reading, with amendments at every stage, and each of them against the United States, and in favor of Collins & Co.! And these are the unprotected, persecuted, suffering individuals, whose *modesty* and *patriotism*, have brought them under the heel of a hard and grasping Government! Commend me to such modesty and patriotism! Of a truth, I know no parallel to them, unless it be found in the standard moderation of those gentle daughters of the horse-leech, whose incessant cry is, "*Give! give!!*"

No one can deny these facts, or dispute the statements I have based upon them. They are from the official records here before me. Contemplate the picture they present! Has Congress been niggardly in its disposition, or hard in its dealings, with this company? Has it not, on the contrary, been liberal to a degree without a parallel in its transactions, and passively complying to every demand? What has it refused? Or, rather, what has it not granted and agreed to, in every particular of terms, time, and money, which this company demanded? Mr. Collins's tongue seems to have been gifted with the spell of "open sesame," to the heart of Congress and the doors of the Treasury; and surely he has not been idle in its use. Three times has he uttered the magic phrase, and as often have we all said "ay," and the public coffers given up their gold. *Cui bono?* What part of the public interest has been promoted by all this? For whose benefit has it all been done? Has it realized the expectations for the public service, upon the hypothesis of which we authorized this contract to be made? Or has it relieved us of these pressing demands upon our time and attention, or saved the Treasury from these perpetual drains? No, sir, no! But, it is a fact beyond dispute, and patent to the world, that this company, themselves, have disregarded the terms of their contract from the beginning; and, in almost every essential particular, have set it at defiance. Its fundamental, and still subsisting, condition has been left out of view; and seems now, indeed, to be impossible of execution. And, at every session, since the thing began, we have been beset by them, with the cry of "help me, Cassius, or I sink!" This cry has come up from the ocean, as if from throats fast filling with the bitter brine; and the other week we heard it gurgling, as if from one going down, for the last time, beneath the tide of near Potomac. Indeed, I never, nowadays, cross the bridge, in walking on the Avenue, without listening for the voice of some drowning Cæsar, from the fetid waters of our own little Tiber. And just as often as we have heard this cry, just so often have we given help. Let us beware, lest the parallel be extended; and ere long we find that we have as little cause as Cassius had, to rejoice in the charity of helping a tyrant to the land. Not that I fear Mr. Collins, or his line, for any direct or immediate mischief he may do, even if he shall get the millions he now demands. No, sir, I have no fears of that. But, there is good cause to fear that, if we recognize the principle which his demand involves, as a rule of action for the Congress, we shall, thereby, have set up a power over us, not less subversive of the principles of the Constitution, and destructive to the just and equal rights of the people, than was the usurpation of Cæsar to the liberties of Rome.

"The contract!" Call you this a contract? By whom has it been recognized as binding? Surely, not by this company. They have not complied with its conditions from the beginning; and they have told us often, *and they tell us now*, they cannot comply with it. Nay, more, that unless we change it, they must give it up. I say this upon authority; at any rate, upon an authority which this company will not dispute, and are bound to recognize. I say it upon the authority of the Senator from New York, [Mr. SEWARD,] who is the *Fidus Achates* and *Ajax* combined, of this company on this floor—their friend in counsel and their champion in fight. In his speech in their behalf, on the 27th of last month, in showing their condition, he said:

"They further show that a capital of $3,000,000 invested has paid no dividends, and been reduced, by inevitable losses, to a little more than $2,500,000; that their stock is sold, in Wall street, at fifty cents on a dollar; *and that, even if they would, yet they cannot dispatch another ship or mail after the 15th of May next.*"

Here, sir, is their confession, in the most direct and emphatic manner, made by their authorized organ and advocate, before the Senate, in the prosecution of their claim. In the face of this confession, call you this a "contract"—a subsisting and binding obligation? Why, sir, it is but the name of such a thing in mockery. It has not one single substantial quality of a valid contract; or, if it ever had, it has been excluded by the purposed violation of one of the parties. *Nihil, nihil!* even as reduced in the derivation, being *ni*-less, *hilum*, than a bean-chaff! Ay, sir, "less and lighter than a bean-chaff;" and blown away by the first breath of reason. It has hardly the form of such an instrument left to commend it to one moment of respect. A contract is reciprocal in its terms, and binding equally upon both parties, or it is no contract at all. When violated by one of the parties, it is, virtually, at an end for both; or, if it be permitted to continue for the benefit of either, it is only at the sufferance of the one who has faithfully observed it. From the moment, then, that this company came before us, and, avowing their inability to execute their part of the contract, asked us to alter its conditions for their relief, it ceased to be binding upon us, and has continued ever since, and is subsisting now, only at our sufferance. At any time since that moment, it has been voidable to us; and we may now, rightfully, declare it absolutely void whenever we think the public interest requires it to be done; and, if we did it in this very hour, the mouth of this company, by their own wrong, is closed forever against a single murmur of complaint.

As will be readily inferred, Mr. President, by all who hear me, I am not a lawyer. To my own consciousness of this, was once added a very sharp reminder, by an eminent member of the bar, when, in a political discussion, he told me that I had learned my *law* from books very different from his. I confessed this to be as true, as that there was an equal difference between the books from which we had, respectively, learned our *politics*. And so I would say now, in anticipation of the musty tomes on "vested rights," which, upon such avowals as I have made, I imagine starting to the memory of certain learned members upon this floor. Sir, if I am not a lawyer—as certainly I am not—I nevertheless have read, with some care, a brief, and to my mind, very comprehensive and conclusive treatise on this doctrine of "vested rights," arising under charters and contracts emanating from Congress. That treatise is from the pens of George Washington, and that body of learned jurists and wise statesmen over whom he presided at Philadelphia, and bears date September 17, 1787. It is entitled "The Constitution of the United States." In that treatise, sir—and it is the fullest and highest authority with me—I find no power in Congress, expressly given, or necessarily implied, to grant charters to individuals, or make contracts with them, of any kind; certainly not to the extent of trammeling the action of any subsequent Congress. Such a power is repugnant to the very genius of the Government that was then forming, and would have been fatally incongruous with all the other provisions of its fundamental law. That genius is *Popular and State representation;* and all those provisions went to secure the freedom and efficiency of its vitality and vigor, by a frequent periodical recurrence to the source of all legitimate power—the *elective franchise*. Without repudiating the very principle upon which they were assembled, and stultifying themselves, the framers of the Constitution could not, as they did not, mar, with such a solecism as the grant of such a power as this, the perfection of those fair tablets of political law they have transmitted to us, and which, in my heart, I religiously believe were, from "the burning bush" of our Revolution, delivered to our fathers, by the hand of Inspiration itself.

I know, sir, but too well, that such considerations as these have often been disregarded, and the great principle I have mentioned has been violated, in the exercise of the very power I deny. Banks, and corporations of an humbler grade, and contracts almost innumerable, lie as thick upon the course of Congressional legislation, as did the black stones along the path of the children of the eastern King, and are just as clamorous when we will not, like those who have preceded us, forget the lessons of the good Dervise, whom we had consulted at the start. I trust there are some here, yet, who will follow the example of those wise children, and stop their ears with leaves from the Constitution; for thus alone will any of us be able to save ourselves, and protect the country, against these dangerous clamors which assail us here, on every side.

But, sir, seeing that the Constitution has thus been disregarded, and that Congress has been so often degraded from its high functions of legislation, and reduced into a mere administrative bureau, what have been the consequences to the country? I appeal to the experienced members of this body—and to you, sir, the most experienced of them all, for the truth of what I say—when I assert that in no instance when such things were done, has the result ever failed to be productive of anything better than disappointment to all good expectations; and mischief, more or less serious and extensive, to the legitimate interests of the country. Beginning with the first charter of the United States Bank, and descending through the whole series of minor monsters and monopolies to this model contract with the Collins line, vary its aspect, and disguise it as you will, the principle you violate is the same; and the evil you do is of the same general character, only less or more in proportion to the degree of force you move it with. This is—it must be so, if God govern his universe by laws.

Pardon me, Mr. President, if such general views as these be somewhat unusual in a speech upon this floor. They lie at the source of all my opinions, whether in law, in medicine, in morals, or in politics. It is my very being to believe that punishment, often swift, sometimes slow, but always certain, follows in the path of wrong, and falls with crushing power upon the violator of any of the laws of the creation, or constitution, of existing things; and has ever done so, from the original sin of our first parents to the last instance when any man has told a lie, in word or deed. Surely, as I have said, the whole history of this Government is strewn thick with proofs of this, as with bleaching bones and still festering forms, is some vast battle-field; and, sad to say, it is as little free from jackals and hyenas, which prowl about it, to feast upon the corrupt and sickening spoils.

But, sir, to come back to particulars. I deny that the Thirtieth or Thirty-first Congress, in the way it has done, had any legitimate power to make this contract with Collins & Co.; and even if it had, that it was binding upon this. So, even if that contract had been kept in good faith, in all respects, by the company; and even if the enterprise it was designed to carry out had been entirely successful in securing all the public benefits it proposed, I deny that there is upon this, the Thirty-second Congress, any constitutionally legal obligation to recognize or consummate it, *because* of its having been a contract with a preceding Congress. Commended to us, if it were, by the propriety of its terms and the practical value of its conditions, we might adopt and continue it during this Congress as a measure of wise expediency. And it is, of course, equally competent for us to repudiate this contract, and refuse to have anything whatever to do with it, if, upon investigation, it is not found worthy of adoption, whether by reason of its inherent defects, or of the bad faith or incompetency of the other parties. I have not time, however, nor is it necessary to my present purpose, to elaborate this view any further.

The question recurs as to the character of the contract itself, the manner in which it has, so far, been executed, and the propriety of continuing it, especially upon the new conditions now proposed.

The leading considerations upon these points, I have already endeavored to present. What I have here to say, relates to somewhat minor and incidental points, which have been suggested by the friends of this measure, in the course of debate.

As a consideration in behalf of this company, and as strongly commending them to our favor, we have been told of the great exertions they have made, and the heavy expenses incurred, first in building their ships, and next in contesting the supremacy of the seas, with the Cunard line, backed by the Treasury of the British Government.

How stands the first item of this account—that is, their exertions and expenses? The contract requires them to build *five* ships. They have built but *four*. In this, then, instead of exceeding, in exertion and expense, what they voluntarily undertook to do—nay, what they begged Congress to permit them to do, and at their own price, they have done and expended *one fifth less*. For building and using in the service of the Government those *five* ships, they were to receive, *and have received*, $385,000 per annum. So they have already, and regularly, received the full amount of compensation, and furnished only *four fifths* of the consideration to which the contracts bind them. They allege that the *four* ships they have built, cost them $3,000,000, or $750,000 each. Then, they have saved the expenditure of that sum, the interest upon which, at six per cent. for two years, is $90,000. I assume two years for this estimate, for the reason, that their contract was made the 1st day of November, 1847, conditioned for the completion of the first *four* ships by the end of *eighteen months*, and the *fifth* one "as early as practicable thereafter." It has now been *four years and a half* since that contract was made. Allowing, then, the contract time for the completion of the first *four* ships, which would have made them ready by the 1st of May, 1849, and then allowing one year more as a sufficient "practicable" time to build the *fifth one*, it leaves a little over two years to this time, that is, from May 1st, 1850, to May 17th, 1852. Upon the $750,000, then, for these two years, during which time it has been withheld from investment, in violation of the contract, the interest amounts, as I said, to $90,000; and this they have saved.

How much they may have saved from other and minor instances of violation of contract, I am unable to ascertain with precision. I learn, however, upon what I deem good authority, that they do not "carry, accommodate, and subsist," as the contract requires, "*four passed midshipmen*, and *one mail agent*, upon each of their ships." And further, that they have not provided *suitable and secure apartments for the mails*, as the contract requires. What would be the sum of these several items of expense, I have no means of estimating with precision. It cannot be less, I apprehend, than several thousand dollars a year. Whatever it may be, however, it is so much saved to them; and, when added to the $90,000 of interest, makes up a sum perhaps not less than $100,000 per annum, which most men, of reasonable desires, in this plain, republican country of ours, would deem a good fortune for a lifetime. But this sum is saved by this company, upon these two items alone, every year, and is either added to their profits, or deducted from their losses. It will be apt to strike a plain man, of common sense, that if $100,000 a year will not cover the losses upon a business, it must be a very "bad business," and ought to be abandoned; or it is in the hands of very "bad managers," and ought to be taken from them.

The sums they have paid for building their ships are set down at a very large amount—$750,000 each. Those who claim to be competent to judge, declare it to be much larger than is either reasonable or sufficient. In proportion to tonnage, these ships have cost much more than the British ships of the same class. Thus, while they exceed the British ships only two hundred tons in size, (which, even at their own estimate of their cost—at $250 a ton—make only $50,000 excess over the British,) they do exceed them $200,000 in cost, or four times the ratio of excess here assumed, which is evidently excessive in itself. This difference cannot be accounted for upon the difference between the prices of labor and materials in the two countries. We know that such a difference does not, in the very nature of things, and cannot exist. I must resort, then, to the only rational, though it may be an extraordinary, explanation which I have been able to find. I am indebted to a friend, a member of this body, for the paper containing it. It is the New York Evening Post of the 8th of this month. The explanation it gives of this matter consists of three short paragraphs. I will read them:

"The Americans can construct and navigate steamers cheaper than they can be constructed and navigated by any other nation. For the accuracy of that statement, we appeal to every disinterested ship-builder on the Atlantic coast, from the Penobscot to the Chesapeake. Why, then, does this company ask twice the aid which is necessary to sustain the Cunard line?

"In the first place, we have the authority of the company for stating that their four steamers cost $3,000,000, while their cash capital amounted only to $1,000,000; so that before they had begun to earn a cent, they were in debt $2,000,000. They were paid for, therefore, mostly in stock; the builders, the engine-makers, the furnishers, all had to take more or less of their pay in stock of the company; in consideration of which they were permitted to put what price they pleased upon their work. This accounts for the Collins vessels costing $200,000 apiece more than the Asia, which is only about two hundred tons less burden, which will average as good time throughout the year as one, if not two, of the Collins steamers, and will carry twice the amount of freight, and nearly twice the number of passengers.

"The Cunard vessels were built for cash at the most favorable cash prices. When launched they did not owe a penny; they were subject to no extortionate charges for interest, and they commenced earning money for their owners the moment they were started, instead of being pledged to pay off mortgages to their builders."

I said this was both reasonable and extraordinary. Is it not so? It is *reasonable*, because it is based upon the statements of the company themselves, and accounts for what is otherwise unaccountable. It is *extraordinary*, else it would be inapplicable to a most extraordinary transaction.

Here we have presented to us a state of things that at first, I confess, astounded me, and almost staggered my belief. It is a lifting of the curtain from a picture which, if one half be true to nature, is alike disgusting in itself, and mortifying in the reflection that we could have had any connection with such a transaction. Here, sir, is one of those "noble enterprises" upon which, as we are so often and so eloquently told, the progress, and prosperity, and honor of our country depends. If this be one of the sources of our progress and prosperity and honor—and perhaps it has received higher praise than any other—then our condition as a people is indeed deplorable; and from all such I pray, in all sincerity, our country may soon be delivered.

But our astonishment, at such an exposition as this, should not result from the character of the transaction itself, for that was to have been expected as the natural result of the hot-bed system of special legislation, which has never given birth to anything better than monsters, or abortions. But the astonishment should be that an American Congress—the representatives of a people more remarkable for common sense than any other in the world—should have been led into this enterprise, and become a partner in this company, expecting success in business, or advantage to the country. Well, the result is now before us. And it, *confessedly*, is a failure of the enterprise, and ruin to the company; and, besides the shame of disappointment, a dead loss of little less than $1,000,000 of the public money; a sum, we had as well, for any good, have thrown to the fishes in the sea.

I do not make this statement at random. I derive the facts from an official source. To insure accuracy, I addressed a letter, last Friday, to the Secretary of the Treasury, inquiring for the entire amount paid, by the United States, to Collins & Co., in cash; and the entire amount received from them, in postages. Here is his answer:

TREASURY DEPARTMENT, *May* 15, 1852.

SIR: I have the honor to inclose herewith a statement from the Sixth Auditor, showing the receipts from the Collins line of steamers, as requested in your letter of yesterday.

A reference to the Navy Department shows the payments to have been $1,039,500, as will appear in detail by referring to Ex. Doc. No. 91, 32d Congress, 1st session, page 3, No payment has been made since 12th February last.

Very respectfully, your obedient servant,

THO. CORWIN,
Secretary of the Treasury.

Hon. SOLON BORLAND, *Senate of the United States.*

The statement of the Sixth Auditor, referred to by the Secretary, is the following, in his letter of the same date:

"The amount of revenue which accrued by the *Collins line alone*, from the 27th April, 1850, to 31st March, 1852, was as follows, viz:

Letter postages	$326,670 58
Newspaper postages	8,560 02
Closed mails	2,104 25
	$337,334 85

In the foregoing statement, the dead letters are not included; but an allowance of $25,322 87 was made in the adjustment of the postal accounts with Great Britain for dead letters received from England by all the lines.

I have the honor to be, very respectfully, your obedient servant, J. W. FARRELLY, *Auditor.*

Hon. THOMAS CORWIN, *Secretary of the Treasury.*

Here, then, it is seen, that while $1,039,500 have been paid to this company by the United States, they have paid back only $337,334, the United States being out of pocket just $702,166. It is a little less than *a million*, as I said, yet it is a very large sum—an enormous sum to be thrown away upon what was a doubtful experiment at first, and is now an exploded scheme.

The item of "dead letter" postage, paid by us to Great Britain, set down at the close of the Auditor's letter at $25,332, I am not sure, from my want of familiarity with such accounts, that I quite understand. I apprehend, however, it is a charge to the expense of transporting the mails. If I am not right in this, the Senator from Texas will correct me. I assume, then, that it is so; and that, relating to "all the lines," as the Auditor says, one half of it, or $12,666, must be added to the account of expense we have paid for the Collins line, and this makes the dead loss to us just $714,832. These are *facts* and *figures* which no one will or can deny. I make this exposition and record of them that they may be heard and seen by those who have to pay these large sums in the way of taxes. Let them be remembered!

In addition to this, we are told here upon this floor, by the best friends of this company—nay, it is one of their pleas for help—that their stock is now selling in the market for *fifty cents on the dollar! Hic jacet!* was never more plainly cut upon the tombstone of any mass of mortality, than this simple statement writes it on the decks of this company of the Collins line.

The honorable Senator from Michigan [Mr. CASS] the other day dwelt upon this fact of the *fifty per cent. discount*, with much emphasis; and assumed, what is certainly true, that the rate thus indicated was the unerring measure of the value of that stock. But there the Senator stopped. Why did he not go a step further in his equation of stock economy, if I may so express it, and assume, as he could have done, with equal truth and much more significance in this connection, that this depreciated price of their stock in the market was the measure and the weight, among sensible men of business, of this company and their enterprise, and the proof, from which there is no escape, that the whole thing is a failure, and a bubble bursted? "*Fifty cents on the dollar!*" Why, sir, it is the very language in which failure is emphatically expressed.

And how could the result be otherwise? Look a moment at the transaction! A speculation, clean, naked, and unredeemed! Upon *one million of money*, this company issued *three millions of stock;* and upon that, bearing interest, they engaged in a pursuit, of which, in view of the result, one of two things must be said: Either the scale upon which it was planned was not required, and could not be sustained by the business of the country; or it has been most shamefully mismanaged. Possibly both may be true, to some extent. How far the first may be, I do not now inquire. I have already shown that there is much truth in the last supposition; and to show this still more clearly and strongly, I have a few more facts, which seem to me to prove that, even had this enterprise been entirely legitimate and well conceived in itself, yet that it has been conducted upon a system of complication and expense, which could not possibly result in anything better than the ruin it has wrought. And added to the inherent viciousness of that system of mismanagement, as if to make success impossible, beyond a doubt, Congress was wheedled into a participation and partnership of this blind and blundering empyricism! An agency, as I have said, which never yet has meddled, but to mar even the wisest plans of individual enterprise.

To show, still further, the miserable mismanagement of this Collins line, I will read, from the same paper, a few of the items of expense of navigating these ships, after incurring, as we have seen, the enormous expense of building and fitting them for service. Here they are:

"By the statement submitted to the Senate committee by Mr. Collins, it appears that the running expense of these steamers is $10 a mile. This is twice as much as is usually allowed by the British Admiralty in their calculations for ocean navigation. They always estimate for a guinea a mile. The cost of running American steamers, we believe, does not generally amount to that, except on the Pacific coast. Here is a difference of half, between the two lines, which it would have been as well for Mr. SEWARD to have directed his attention to, before he made his imaginary trip with his brother Senators to St. Stephen's Chapel. Here is a difference just covering the depreciation, which, he says, the Collins stock has experienced in finding its level in Wall street. If the imaginative Senator had spent less time in getting up his rhetoric, and more at getting at the material facts in the case he attempts to discuss, he would probably have done what, for his own sake, we wish General CASS had done.

* * * * * * * * * *

"He would have inquired, as we have done, the cause of this extraordinary expense of running the Collins steamers, and he would have learned, as we have learned, that it is not one which it becomes the United States, or any other Government, to countenance or encourage.

"We happen to have the means of comparing some of the expenses of running the two rival lines, and we propose to submit the facts to the public, in the hope that they will have some influence upon those whose support of this monopoly does not originate in other considerations than those which are addressed to their reason or their patriotism.

"The following estimate of the cost of running the two lines was made up, we have reason to believe, and do believe, from the books of the two companies:

	Collins.	*Cunard.*	
Cost of the Baltic . $700,000			
Cost of the Asia... 500,000			
Pay-roll for two months....	$9,000	$5,400	
Consumption of coal a round voyage ....2,000 tons	10,000		
" " 1,400 tons	-	7,000	
Ins 6 pr ct pr ann. } Depreciation 8 per cent. } for 2 ms Repairs 6 per ct. }	23,333	16,666	
	$42,333	$29,066	
Excess of Collins's expenditure per ship...........	-	-	$13,267
Or for 4 ships for 26 voyages	-	-	$345,042

"It may be objected that the Collins ships are larger than the Asia, and therefore more expensive to run. The difference is only about two hundred tons, not enough to increase the expense materially, and besides, the rate of increase in the expense of running steamships is always inversely as the tonnage, and, therefore, even if the difference were material, it would not strengthen the application of the Collins company.

"Here we have a difference of $345,042 annually—a sum equal, within about $5,000, to the entire allowance of the British Government to the Cunard company. Among the items on the pay-roll, there is one worthy of a specific reference. The Cunard captains receive, all round, $2,500 a year. The captains of the Collins steamers receive $6,000—difference, $3,500 on each ship. The reason of this difference is, as we are told, that the Collins captains are obliged to own a quantity of the stock of the company ($30,000 worth is the amount we have heard stated) before they can receive a commission.

"That being the case, they certainly have not been overpaid thus far, if, as we presume, they bought at par; but it is none the less extravagant and wasteful in the company to do their business in such a way as to be obliged at the very commencement of their enterprise to pay people in their company to take their stock—for a portion of these salaries can be looked upon in no other light—and to saddle the stockholders with the expense."

These facts need no comment, to answer the purpose for which I have introduced them. They show the true character of this company, and put the seal of condemnation, beyond escape, upon all their operations. They commenced without capital, and have conducted themselves throughout as wild and reckless speculators—speculators upon individual credit and credulity, and upon the faith of this Government.

My honorable friend from Kentucky [Mr. UNDERWOOD] will find in these statements I have read, something like a solution of the questions which puzzled even his arithmetic the other day. When he made his calculations then, I suppose he estimated the payments to be in cash, and therefore put all the items down at the standard of a cash valuation. He did not then know that those payments were made in *stocks depreciated to fifty cents on the dollar.* So, if he was puzzled over his arithmetic then, because its relentless rules would not carry the legitimate amount of expense up to the enormous sum set down by the company, I apprehend that the straight-forward honesty of his mind will be even more amazed now, at the *cause* of the difficulty, than he was puzzled then, at the difficulty itself. Now, sir, as practical questions to a practical man, I ask my friend from Kentucky, what would be thought of a company in his State who should engage in business (no matter how legitimate and promising in itself) upon a capital two thirds of which was borrowed at interest; and then, in the prosecution of that business, should undertake to pay all its expenses by selling its own paper in the market at *fifty cents on the dollar?* How long could such a company sell its paper at all? How long could it obtain credit at all? Would any sensible man among his constituents take stock in such a company, or become in any way connected with it? Would not the undivided sentiment of the community be, that there was ridiculous folly or deep knavery at the bottom of the whole concern? Well, sir, it seems to me this is a case in point. If there be any material difference between them, in a practical point of view, I am unable to perceive or appreciate it. But it is said, I am aware, that I and a few others here do not take "broad, statesmanlike, national views" of such questions as this. And I trust I never shall, if in doing so, as in this case, I must repudiate my principles and the common sense which the God of my creation has endowed me with.

But even this extraordinary cause of increased expenditure for two months, or a trip, as set forth in the paper I have read, does not carry the amount up to the $65,000, as stated by the company. But it makes only $42,333; although this estimates for the Collins pay-roll $9,000, while the Cunard is but $5,000; for the Collins coal bill $10,000, while the Cunard is but $7,500; and for the Collins insurance, depreciation, and repairs $23,333, while the Cunard is but $16,666—total Collins $42,333—total Cunard $29,066. Here is an excess, yet, of $13,267 per trip, to be accounted for. Perhaps some light may be thrown upon this, if any one can or will answer certain interrogatories which I will here propound. Perhaps if the Senator from New Jersey [Mr. MILLER] were here, he might, from the familiarity with the subject he evinced by his speech some weeks ago; or, at any rate, I have no doubt that the Senator from New York [Mr. SEWARD] could furnish us an answer from that rich budget of facts with which he seemed prepared the other day, and of which he gave us a glimpse so curious. But, whether I can have them answered here or not, I will now propound them, and then put them in my printed speech, so that some one else may answer them for the information of the country, if not of the Senate. We want light. Here are the interrogatories:

1. Who are the shareholders in the company owning the Collins line of ocean steamers, and where do they reside?

2. What commission is charged by Brown & Brothers, the British agents, per voyage, or per annum, for their services to this line?

3. What extra prices, above the current market prices, are paid for disbursements, provisions, and outfits at Liverpool?

4. What commissions are charged by Collins at New York for his services to the line?

5. Do not the expenses, on these accounts, amount to more than $13,000 a trip?

6. Is not this line mortgaged to a member of the British Parliament for $700,000?

7. Where are the insurances effected, and at what rates? Where is the coal purchased, and at what prices? What is the difference between those prices and the prices paid by the Cunard line? Where are the officers and crews employed, and are they paid at American or English prices, and what is the difference?

Then there are a few questions I asked the Senator from New York [Mr. SEWARD] the other day in debate, which he has not answered, and which I will now repeat. I hope he, or some other competent person, will answer them at their convenience. That Senator then said that—

"The insurance on the Cunard line of steamships, valued at $500,000, at three per cent. in England, is.... $15,000
Insurance of the Collins line of steamships, valued at $700,000, at six per cent., is............ 42,000
The total insurance on the Collins line is......... 168,000
The total insurance on the Cunard line is........ 60,000
Making a difference against the Collins line of.... 108,000
"The rate of wages for the persons employed as captains, engineers, and common seamen, is about one third higher in this country than in England."

I copy this from his printed speech. When he made it, I asked him if I heard aright, and if that statement could be true? I asked him if it could be true of two companies, each running a line of ships of the same character, upon the same ocean, to and from the same ports—engaged in the same kind of business—having access to the same markets for similar materials, labor, supplies, money, and insurance—that one was in anywise compelled to pay, or *did*, actually, pay double, or even a third, over the rates and prices that the other paid, upon all, or any one of those items, as he had set it forth? I asked the questions in good faith; for the statement struck me as so extraordinary, that I was not sure I heard the Senator correctly. He did not answer me then; but as he has put the same statement in print, I take that as *his* answer. Let my questions and this answer go to the public together. I submit it to the practical sense of men of business, that if the Senator's statement be true, that Collins & Co. do pay these excessive prices, when lower ones are at their option, their business is either grossly mismanaged for want of sense, or want of honesty. *Compete* with the British, indeed! At such a rate, and by such a system, we cannot pay them money enough to enable them to *compete*. We might enable them to go on; but it would be at the expense of both the interest and honor of the country. It would be no competition, but a miserable scramble for a premium upon incompetency or corruption. I do not believe a word of it. And, most assuredly, I will never countenance or sustain such a state of things, if it be true, by any vote of mine.

Again: we are told that we must sustain this Collins line, *because* the British Government sustains the Cunard line. Even as a general proposition, I do not admit this to be true. But I will not discuss that further than I have done in another portion of my remarks. Admitting it, however, for the argument, though not in fact, I yet deny that such a consideration gives any force or validity to the claim for this increased allowance, now made by the Collins line. It is a fact, beyond dispute, that in this matter of following the example of the British Government, and giving large compensation to our steamers, because she gives large compensation to hers, we are not only not behind, but we have already *exceeded her*, in the rate of compensation allowed. We already pay Collins several thousand dollars more, per trip, than Great Britain pays Cunard for similar service. Thus, we pay Collins $19,000, while Cunard receives from his Government but $15,000; the excess in favor of Collins being $4,000 per trip, or $96,000 per annum.

I know, sir, we are told that the British Government has latterly increased the compensation of the Cunard line from £145,000 to £175,000 per annum. But I have not seen sufficient evidence to satisfy me that this is true. The only evidence we have, about which there seems to be no doubt on this point, gives the £145,000 as the annual compensation, which makes about $15,000 per trip. We are told that a *Mr. Livingston*, who seems to be one of the Collins Company, or is deeply interested with it, has said that this had been increased to £175,000. Gentlemen may take this as evidence of the increase of British compensation, who choose to do so. To me it has so far appeared only as a vague rumor, the truth of which no Senator here seems willing to vouch for. It is also from an interested source, and offered as aid to a certain end. Of the individual who offers it I know nothing. I neither admit nor deny the truth of his statement. The amount which I have assumed, I find stated in a book of unquestioned authority for facts of this kind—"The British Almanac, for 1851." On page 63, in the article on "North American Mails," I find the following:

"It was in the autumn of 1845 that the negotiations were going on; and in the spring of next year the new contract was completed, by virtue of which the Cunard Company undertake to dispatch a mail steamer once a fortnight from Liverpool to Halifax and Boston, and another mail steamer once a fortnight from Liverpool to New York, the price being £145,000 per annum, and the contract to remain in force till 1858."

I find nothing on this point later, or different, in any official document, or from any other reliable source. This, moreover, is admitted on all hands to be true. But suppose it to be true, that this increase of £175,000 has been given to the Cunard line. It does not materially affect the argument. It still leaves the compensation to the Cunard line a little short of $18,000 per trip; while the Collins line still receive the $19,000, or $1,000 per trip more than the British line. There is no established truth, therefore, in this part of the plea; and even if there was, it has no force nor validity whatever. Instead of sustaining this claim, then, it is directly against it.

These are facts which are indisputable. In view of them, what becomes of this plea of the necessity of sustaining the Collins line, against the patronage of the British Government? Gone, sir; gone, like mist before the morning sun. Protection of American enterprise against British gold! That is the demand. And all who do not at once concede it, are charged with want of patriotism. And yet the facts, here staring us in the face, prove beyond dispute, that we have not merely given this protection—not merely placed the American ships on an equal footing with the British—but we have *done more*, sir. We have given them *more money* and *more protection*. And now they demand still more—nay, nearly double as much. They already receive (at the highest estimate for the British) $19,000, while the British receive but $18,000; and now they demand $33,000, or an increase of $14,000 a trip upon what they now receive, or $15,000 a trip *more* than the British ships receive! Call you this American enterprise? Call you this American competiton with British energy and British skill! Why, sir, it is but a game of bragg, with stakes of gold, the party winning who has the heavier purse. "This is not the entertainment to which we were invited." We came not here to gamble—certainly not with the public money. And yet, sir, if this be not so, in what attitude does such a proposition as the amendment makes place us before the world? It has ever been our boast, and it is one which every American heart may make with an honest pride, that "give us but daylight and fair play," and American enterprise, arts, and arms can stand against the world, and win a glorious triumph everywhere. And our history proves it to be not unfounded. Upon no battle-field, whether in arts or arms, from our national birthday to the present hour, even with the odds against us, have we ever been defeated. The amount of money our Government might collect, and expend in magnificent display, has never been the subject of a boast from any true American heart. It never will be. That money, under the genius of our institutions, is better in the pockets of the people; so much of it as may be needed for a just and equal administration, and for defense, being ready, as we all know, to be poured with freedom into the public coffers, at a moment's notice; and no more than that should be given.

But, sir, this amendment declares that ours is an empty boast. It declares, in words which cannot be mistaken nor misunderstood, that American enterprise and skill *cannot* stand against the British upon equal terms—nay, not even when we have the advantage of a heavier purse. The confession is there made—ay, sir, there it stands upon the table before you, in the official records of the nation. If it be true, its tortuous lines should be taken from that table, and, by some British loom, woven into a veil, as black as the ink in which they are traced upon the record, to hang forever upon these bold American faces of ours, in this day of our national humiliation!

Sir, if I thought it true, I never would, I never could again, as an American citizen, hold up my head, in pride of my native land. I never would assert again that America was the equal of any other nation in the world. But, on my knees, I would go down before that strong Genius of American enterprise and skill, of whom we hear so much, and pray him to strike the galling libel from our escutcheon, and swear by him who spoke this glorious land of ours into being, that no hand should ever write it there again. But, sir, it is not true. As an American, I swear it. We *are* able to stand against the world, without the heavier purse—without adventitious aid from any quarter. Even when the odds have been against us, as they always have upon the ocean, we have been successful in every encounter, and have gone on prospering and to prosper, while competing with every nation, upon every sea. Sir, no instance can be cited in which it ever was pretended that success had failed us, *until the coming of this Collins line*. But, tell me not that such a thing as that, truly represents the enterprise, or skill, or talent, or spirit, of our countrymen. No, sir, no! It is a false heir—a miserable pretender—a monster, begot by folly on corruption, sent from some dark abode below to degrade us before the world; or, if by decree of Heaven, surely sent to chastise us for our sins, and move us to repentance. Mark its coming with the blackest stone the calendar affords; but not, I protest, as a sign of our people's degeneration and decay.

No, sir; the day of our declination in the great cycle of time has not yet come. My trust in God is, that, high already as we have climbed the sky, in progress and prosperity, the point of our culmination is yet far higher and further away; and that we, and our children, and our children's children, and generations to come after them, shall not see that highest point attained; but that our country's course shall be onward and upward, as long as time shall last.

Mr. President, my strength again has failed me. I know, also, that the Senate is fatigued with a long sitting, and is anxious to adjourn. While, therefore, there are several other points in this question of interest to me, and particularly one of special interest to my constituents, which I have been unable to reach, I shall seek another opportunity to present my views upon those points, if my health permit, before the question shall be finally disposed of. For the present, I have no more to say.

AMERICAN STEAM NAVIGATION.

SPEECH

OF

WILLIAM H. SEWARD,

FOR

THE COLLINS STEAMERS.

IN SENATE OF THE UNITED STATES, APRIL 27, 1852.

WASHINGTON, D. C.
BUELL & BLANCHARD, PRINTERS.
1852.

AMERICAN STEAM NAVIGATION.

SPEECH

OF

WILLIAM H. SEWARD,

FOR

THE COLLINS STEAMERS.

IN SENATE OF THE UNITED STATES, APRIL 27, 1852.

WASHINGTON, D. C.
BUELL & BLANCHARD, PRINTERS.
1852.

SPEECH.

Mr. President :

What will Congress do—what has Congress done—for the Collins steamers? These are questions which meet every visiter returning from the Capital on his arrival at New York, and which every traveller from America encounters, on Change in Liverpool and London, and in the Courts of Paris and St. Petersburg. There is reason enough for all this curiosity and interest among the merchants and statesmen of the two continents.

Mr. President, under a contract with the United States made on the 19th of April, 1849, between E. K. Collins, James Brown, and Stewart Brown, merchants of New York, and the United States, those persons now prosecute, between the ports of New York and Liverpool, forty voyages across the ocean, or twenty outward and inward voyages, annually, in steamships carrying freights and passengers on their own account, and also public mails on account of the United States, and receive from the Treasury, as a compensation for that service, three hundred and eighty-five thousand dollars a year, which is equivalent to somewhat more than $19,000 for each outward and return passage. The Committee on Finance propose an amendment to the annual Deficiency bill, the effect of which is to increase the number of mails and voyages from twenty to twenty-six, and the compensation from $19,000 to $33,000 for each voyage.

Ought this measure to be adopted?

I assume, for the present, that the existing enterprise is to be perseveringly sustained. In that view the question arises—

Whether the proposed increase of mail service is expedient.

When this line was established, the British Cunard steamers, consisting of seven vessels, were making semi-monthly voyages and carrying semi-monthly mails between the same ports during the eight temperate months, and monthly mails during the four other months; and thus they had a monopoly of steam ocean postage between the two countries. We authorized the Collins line to carry just the same number of mails, alternating with the Cunard steamers; and so we broke up the monopoly, and divided the postages of the route equally with Great Britain. So far, all was right and well. But recently the Cunard steamers have continued their semi-monthly mails throughout the whole year, while ours were limited to the eight temperate months; and so the equality of postage revenues has been subverted, and the early British monopoly has been partially restored. By the proposed increase of mails we shall exactly alternate again; and on every day that an American or European mail steam-vessel shall leave New York, one of the other line will leave the opposite port; and so the monopoly will again be broken, and the complete equality of postage revenues will be re-established. We must do just this, or relinquish in an important degree the great postal object of the enterprise. The Postmaster General and the Secretary of the Navy, and the Senate's Committees on the Post Office, on Naval Affairs, and on Finance, agree that the service must be thus increased, if it is to be at all continued. The increase, then, is not merely expedient, but even necessary and indispensable.

Assuming now that the service is to be increased, the question comes up—

Is the increase of compensation from $19,000 *to* $33,000 *per voyage just and reasonable?*

It *is* just and reasonable, if *necessary*. It is clear that some increase is necessary. The proprietors decline to make the six new voyages for nothing, and even to make them for $19,000 a voyage. We cannot oblige the contractors to make them for that compensation, nor even to make them for any compensation, for they are beyond the contract. No one else offers to make them on those terms, or, indeed, on any terms. We must therefore apply to Mr. Collins and his associates to enlarge the contract. But opening the contract for enlargement opens it for revision. They consent to enlarge, but they equally appeal to us to remodel it; and they show for reasons, that while the average cost of each

voyage is - - - - - - - - - - - - -	$65,216.64
The average receipts are only - - - -	48,286.85
And that they incur an average loss of -	16,928.79
And an aggregate loss annually of - -	$338,574.40

They further show that a capital of three millions invested has paid no dividends, and been reduced by inevitable losses to a little more than two and a half millions; that their stock is sold in Wall street at fifty cents on a dollar; and that, even if they would, yet they cannot despatch another ship or mail after the 15th of May next. Something must be allowed, if not for profits, at least for renovation; and so the actual loss on each voyage being in round numbers $17,000, it is quite certain that an increase of not less than $19,000 is necessary to keep the steamers in vigorous and sure operation.

All questions of the fairness of this showing are precluded by the offer of the contractors to relinquish the enterprise to the United States, or to any assignee indicated by them, after the contract shall have been remodelled, and by the neglect of any other party to propose for a new contract, even on the terms thus recommended.

So, the increase of compensation solicited is just and reasonable, and is, moreover, like the increase of the mail service, necessary and indispensable.

Now, sir, we have arrived at the very question of the whole question. We must do just what is thus proposed, or relinquish the contract altogether.

The honorable Chairman of the Committee on Finance, [Mr. Hunter,] dissenting from his associates, advises that alternative. Sir, with a profound respect for that distinguished Senator, not now for the first time, nor for mere effect, expressed, I must have his pardon, nevertheless, for preferring the authority of his associates. Extreme caution is apt to be the fruit of the patient and patriotic labors of his office. An appropriation bill seldom has passed this House without calling forth from him or his predecessors eloquent, yet groundless, alarms of an exhausted treasury, and of impending taxation, if not bankruptcy.

While we cannot, without wounding the national sensibilities and impairing the national character, abandon any great enterprise, it is equally true that indecision is among the worst vices of the statesman, and that vacillation in the conduct of public affairs is fruitful of national demoralization, and indicative of certain national decline. Persistence, when practicable, invigorates national energies, discourages foreign rivalry, and prevents foreign insult and aggression. Compare France—enlightened, vigorous, and energetic, but unstable as water—with England, cautious, constant, and persevering, or even with Russia, unimpassioned and cold as her climate, yet with her eyes unswervingly and forever fixed on Stamboul, and you have an apt illustration of my moral. Nevertheless, these general observations are inconclusive, and I grapple therefore cheerfully, with this great question.

If this enterprise must be abandoned, it must be for one of two reasons, namely: either because—

1. *It was erroneously conceived; or because*, 2. *It has been rendered unnecessary, unwise, or impracticable, by subsequent events and circumstances.*

1. *Was it erroneously conceived?* To determine this question, we need to ascend some high eminence of time, from which we can look back along the past, and pierce,

as far as is allowed to human vision, through the clouds and darkness that rest upon the future. Come, then, Senators, and suppose that you stand with me in the galleries of St. Stephen's Chapel on a day so long gone by as the 22d of March, 1775. A mighty debate has been going on here in this august Legislature of the British Empire. Insurrection against commercial restriction has broken out in the distant American colonies; a seditious assembly in Philadelphia has organized it; and a brave, patient, unimpassioned, and not untried soldier of Virginia, lies, with hastily gathered and irregular levies, on the heights of Dorchester, waiting the coming out of the British army from Boston. The question whether Great Britain shall strike, or concede and conciliate, has just been debated and decided. Concession has been denied. A silence, brief but intense, is broken by the often fierce and violent, but now measured and solemn, utterance of Burke: "My counsel has been rejected. You have determined to trample upon and extinguish a people who have, in the course of a single life, added to England as much as she had acquired by a progressive increase of improvement, brought on, by varieties of civilizing conquests and civilizing settlements, in a series of seventeen hundred years. A vision has passed before my eyes; the spirit of prophecy is upon me. Listen, now, to a revelation of the consequences which shall follow your maddened decision. Henceforth there shall be division, separation, and eternal conflict in alternating war and peace between you and the child you have oppressed, which has inherited all your indomitable love of liberty and all your insatiable passion for power. Though still in the gristle, and not yet hardened into the bone of manhood, America will, within the short period of sixteen months, cast off your dominion and defy your utmost persecution. Perfecting the institutions you have not yet suffered to ripen, she will establish a republic, the first confederate representative commonwealth, which shall in time become the admiration and envy of the world. France, the hereditary rival whom, only twenty years ago, with the aid of your own colonies, you despoiled of her North American possessions, though they had been strengthened by the genius of Richelieu, will take sweet revenge in aiding the emancipation of those very colonies, and thus dismembering your empire. You will strike her in vain with one hand, while you stretch forth the other to reduce your colonies with equal discomfiture. And you, even you, most infatuated yet most loyal prince, will within eight years sign a treaty of peace with the royal Bourbon, and of independence with republican America! With fraud, corruption, fire, and sword, you will compensate England with conquests in the East, and within half a century they will surround the world, and the British flag shall wave over provinces covering five millions of square miles, and containing one-sixth of the inhabitants of the globe. Nor shall you lose your retaliation upon your ancient enemy; for she, in the mean time, imbibing and intoxicated by the spirit of revolution in her American affiliation, shall overthrow all authority, human and divine, and, exhausting herself by twenty-five years of carnage and desolation throughout continental Europe, shall at last succumb to your victorious arms, and relapse, after ineffectual struggles, into the embraces of an inglorious military despotism. Yet, notwithstanding all these unsurpassed conquests and triumphs, shall you enjoy no certain or complete dominion. For, on the other hand, wild beasts and savage men and uncouth manners shall all disappear on the American continent; and the three millions whom you now despise, gathering to themselves increase from every European nation and island, will, within seventy-five years, spread themselves over field and forest, prairie and mountain, until, in your way to your provinces in the Bahamas, they shall meet you on the shores of the Gulf of Mexico, and on your return from the Eastern Indies, they will salute you from the Eastern coast of the Pacific ocean. In the mean time, with genius developed by the influence of freedom, and with vigor called forth and disciplined in the subjugation of the forest and trained and perfected in the mysteries of ship-building and navigation, by the hardy exercise of the whale fisheries under either pole, they will, in all European conflicts, with keen sagacity, assume the relation of neutrals, and thus grasp the prize of Atlantic commerce dropped into their hands by fierce belligerents. In the midst of your studies and experiments in hydraulics, steam, and electricity, they will seize the unpracticed and even incomplete inventions, and cover their rivers with steamboats, and connect and bind together their widely separated Territories with canals, railroads, and telegraphs. When a long interval of peace shall have come, your merchants, combining a vast capital, will regain and hold for a time the carrying trade, by substituting capacious, buoyant, and fleet packet-ships, departing and arriving with exact punctuality; but the Americans, quickly borrowing the device and improving on your skill, will reconquer their commerce. You will then rouse all the enterprise of your merchants, and all the spirit of your Government, and wresting the new and mighty power of steam from the hands of your inveterate rival, will apply it to ocean navigation, and laying hold of the commercial and social correspondence between the two continents, increasing as the nations rise to higher civilization and come into more close and intimate relations, as the basis of postal revenue, you will thus restore your lost monopoly on the Atlantic, and enjoy it unmolested through a period of ten years. During that season of triumph, you will mature and perfect all the arrangements for extending this mighty device of power and revenue, so as to connect every island of the seas and every part of every continent with your capital. But just at that moment your emulous rival will appear with steamships still more capacious, buoyant, and fleet, than your own, in your harbors, and at once subverting your Atlantic monopoly, will give earnest of her vigorous renewal of the endless contest for supremacy of all the seas. When you think her expelled from the ocean, her flag will be seen in your ports, covering her charities contributed to relieve your population, stricken by famine; and while you stand hesitating whether to declare between republicanism and absolute power in continental Europe, her ambassadors will be seen waiting on every battle-field to salute the triumphs of liberty; and when that cause shall be overthrown, the same constant flag shall be seen even in the Straits of the Dardanelles, receiving with ovations due to conquerors the temporarily overthrown champions of freedom. Look towards Africa, there you see American colonies lifting her up from her long night of barbarism into the broad light of liberty and civilization. Look to the East, you see American missionaries bringing the people of the Sandwich Islands into the family of nations, and American armaments peacefully seeking yet firmly demanding the rights of humanity in Japan. Look to the Equator, there are American engineers opening passages by canals and railroads across the isthmus which divides the two oceans. And last of all, look Northward, and you behold American sailors penetrating the continent of ice in search of your own daring and lost navigators."

Sir, this stupendous vision has become real. All this momentous prophecy has come to pass. The man yet lives who has seen both the end and the beginning of its fulfilment. It is history. And that history shows that this enterprise of American Atlantic steam navigation was wisely and even necessarily undertaken, to maintain our present commercial independence, and the contest for the ultimate empire of the ocean. Only a word shall express the importance of these objects. International postal communication and foreign commerce are as important as domestic mails and traffic. Equality with other nations in respect to those interests is as important as freedom from restriction upon them among ourselves. Except Rome—which substituted conquest and spoliation for commerce—no nation was ever highly prosperous, really great, or even truly independent, whose foreign communications and traffic were conducted by other States; while Tyre, and Egypt, and Venice, and the Netherlands, and Great Britain, successively becoming the merchants, became thereby the masters of the world.

But the learned and honorable Chairman of the Committee on Finance raises a question on a warlike feature of the enterprise which has not yet come under our notice. Departing, after the most profound consideration, from the ancient naval policy which separated the National Ocean Police from the National Mercantile Marine, Great Britain constructs all the steamships employed in her postal service; so that they are "good, substantial, and efficient—of such model and strength as to be fit and able to carry guns of the largest caliber used on board of her Majesty's steam-vessels of war," and they are subject to be taken in emergencies by the Government, at cost, for the public naval service. And in this way Great Britain is rapidly and steadily building up a new and peculiar naval force, which will always be in complete condition and ready for effective use. The same principle was adopted in the contract with Collins and his associates; and the evidence is complete that it has been faithfully and fully carried out. The honorable Senator now disputes the soundness of the principle itself, and insists that merchant steam-vessels cannot be constructed so as to be practically useful for warlike purposes. I reply, first, that having, on such careful examination and with such weighty example, adopted the principle, we could not now wisely abandon it, without proof, by practical trial, long I hope to be delayed, that it is erroneous. Secondly: No ship of war, however constructed, is adapted to all the exigencies of naval service, while these steamships are certainly adapted to some of them. Commodore Perry, on the 15th of February, 1852, reports to the Secretary of the Navy that "these steamships (of the Collins line) may be converted, at an expense of $20,000 each, into war steamers of the first class; and that each of them could carry four 10-inch Paixhan guns on pivots, fore and aft, of the weight of those in the model ship Mississippi, and ten 8-inch Paixhan guns on the sides, and that this armament would not incommode the vessel; and that, in the general operations of a maritime war, they would render good service; and especially that, from their great speed, they would be useful as despatch vessels and for the transportation of troops, being always capable of attack and defence, and of overhauling and escaping from an enemy."

The Secretary of War reports to the Senate, on the 20th of March, 1852, that "the readiness of the steamers to be used at the shortest notice, their capacity of being used as transports for goods and munitions of war, and their great celerity of motion, enabling them to overhaul merchantmen, and at the same time escape cruisers, would render them terrible as guerrillas of the ocean."

Thirdly. Great Britain has already more than two hundred and fifty steamers, armed and capable of armament. What would be our situation, in the emergency of a war, if we were unprovided with a similar force for defence and aggression?

But, fourthly. The warlike adaptation of the steamers is a collateral and contingent feature of the enterprise, which will stand safely on the accomplishment of its postal and mercantile ends, even if that feature should prove valueless. These steamers, at least, are built and in use, and accomplish their important civic purposes. We may correct our system, not in this, but in future operations.

Thus, Mr. President, it appears that the enterprise was wisely adopted. And now I pray you take notice that *it has not been rendered unwise or impracticable by any change of circumstances or of public interests.* Everything in these respects remains as it was, except that we have increased ability and increased need to put it forth in the struggle for the freedom of commerce and the command of the seas.

Nor does the expense complained of affect the question of perseverance. The excess of expense above the estimates results from the wise policy of building larger and better ships than were at first contemplated, whereby in achievement we have not merely equalled but surpassed Great Britain.

Nor is the expense of the American steamers disproportionate to that of the British. Although we all know that for a time it might well be so, because the rate of interest, and the cost of labor and of skill, are higher on this side of the Atlantic than on the other, and because higher insurance must be paid on more valuable vessels. Nevertheless, the Cunard steamers, seven in number, have an aggregate capacity of 12,252 tons, averaging 1,750 tons for each, and they cross the Atlantic eighty-five times annually ; thus the whole tonnage worked by them across the Atlantic is 148,750 tons.

The Collins steamers have an aggregate tonnage of 13,700, averaging 3,425 tons for each; and the aggregate tonnage worked by them across the ocean is 178,100 tons ; the cost to the Government is $850,000, not exceeding, in proportion to their work, the expense of the Cunard line. At the same time, they excel the Cunard steamers in speed. The shortest westward passage of the Cunard steamers was ten days and twenty-two hours, and the shortest eastward passage ten days and twelve hours; while the quickest westward passage of the Collins steamers was nine days and twelve hours, and the quickest eastward passage was nine days and eight hours.

Nor is the expense disproportioned to the benefits received. The first effect of the enterprise was a postal treaty with Great Britain; and under that treaty, in lieu of receiving no steam ocean postages, as before, we now receive postages amounting in round numbers to $400,000; and this revenue must swell, and is actually swelling, at the rate of $200,000 annually. Thus, in the first place, it is clear that in two years the postal revenue alone will defray the expense; and, secondly, there lies very near to us in the future what my friend from Massachusetts [Mr. SUMNER] so justly denominates, and what every patriot and philanthropist so earnestly seeks, the great boon of cheap ocean postage.

And now, while we maintain postal communication to every part of our country, at no matter how great expense, provided that the revenue of the whole system shall equal the cost of all its parts, I desire to know why we should depart from a principle so enlightened in foreign postal conventions, which are ancillary to commerce, to immigration, and to political influence and power. But if we change the terms of the question, it will be more easily solved. What, then, shall we lose by arresting the enterprise? We shall lose all the postages on steam mails, and all the hopes of cheap postage, and all the profits on passengers and freight transported by steam. It is not easy to estimate these losses; but we have some knowledge of the profits of Great Britain, arising from the monopoly she enjoyed before our competition. The duties received into the treasury from the Cunard steamers rose in six years from $73,809 to $1,054,731. She paid the steamers for carrying the mails six years $2,550,000, and received postages in return amounting to $7,836,800; giving her a clear profit, on the postal revenue, of $5,286,800, or little less than a million a year. We have gained at least one-half of what benefits Great Britain has lost by reason of our enterprise. Let that monopoly be restored and re-established, we shall then lose all that gain, and with it we shall see the postages, and freights, and rates of passage, raised to their ancient standards, and continually adjusted equally to injure our prosperity and promote the interests and gratify the caprice of Great Britain. What shall we then look for but decline of trade and industry, with a long train of commercial embarrassments and national humiliations?

At most, we can save by abandoning this enterprise only about $300,000 in two years. Could we not now easily retrench to that extent in some other quarter? We can save as much, and more, by laying up one of our frigates in ordinary during the same time, and twice as much by burning it down to the water's edge. No one would advise this, and yet it would be far less disastrous than the retrenchment now proposed.

Still, sir, the argument that the expense exceeds the estimates is pressed. Well, there is nothing new in that. This is a deficiency bill. It makes appropriations of some millions to supply deficiencies in the customs service, in the construction of public edifices, in the improvement and embellishment of the capital, in the department of Indian Affairs, in the department of the Territories, and in the department of Foreign Relations. And just such a deficiency bill comes up from the House of Representatives, at the middle of every session of Congress, as punctually as the estimates for the year come in at the beginning, and as the appropriation bill based on these estimates appears at the close. Shall we, then, abandon the customs, the public edifices, the seat of Government, the army and navy, the Indian tribes, the Territories, and all foreign intercourse, because we can never estimate accurately, at the beginning, the cost of maintaining them throughout the fiscal year?

But it is said that the enterprise is a departure from the principle of free trade. Sir, it is a departure from that principle, but not a divergence from the fixed and ancient policy of the country. Widely, and I think unwisely, as we have differed among ourselves about the policy of protecting agriculture and manufactures, to the hindrance of the growth of commerce itself, yet we have, from first to last, uncompromisingly and unwaveringly adhered to the policy of protecting navigation. We inherited it from England, whose navigation act, passed by the Long Parliament, and co-operating with her encouragement of manufactures, broke the monopoly of Holland, and secured to the British islands the commerce of the world and the command of the ocean. If this measure enhances protection of our navigation, it is because British largesses enhance the protection of her navigation. Let her revert to her old measure of protection, and we can at once safely return to ours.

The honorable Senator from Virginia tells us that it is wise to give up now, because, the system being unprofitable, we shall be obliged to give up at last. But this is only a temporary contest, not yet fully decided, and growing in success. Collins's contract has eight years to run. Long before that time, Atlantic steam navigation will prove itself to be either self-sustaining or not self-sustaining. In either case, Great Britain will withdraw her patronage from her line, and we can then safely discontinue our contributions to our line.

The honorable Senator from Virginia seeks to divide us on this question, by presenting the claims of what he calls the poorer cities for a share in the benefits of this policy, now concentrated upon New York. I learn that a bill is near its third reading in the Legislature of the Old Dominion, having for its object to establish a line of first-class steamships between Norfolk and Antwerp. Sir, I assure the honorable Senator that when a proposition shall come before us for material aid to the trade of any of our Atlantic cities, which shall at the same time be beneficent to the whole Union—whether that city be Boston, or Philadelphia, or Baltimore, or Norfolk, or Charleston, or New Orleans—I shall greet it with no reluctant hearing. But in the mean time the field of battle is chosen, not by us, but by the enemy; it is not a provincial contest for provincial objects, but it is a national one. We must meet our adversary on that field, not elsewhere; and we must meet him or surrender the whole nation's cause without a blow.

And now I pray honorable Senators to consider what it is that we are invited to surrender. It is no less than the proud commercial and political position we have gained by two wars with Great Britain, and by the vigorous and well-directed enterprise of our countrymen through a period now reaching to three-quarters of a century.

Next, I pray you to consider what position we must

take after that surrender—the position of Mexico, of the Canadas, and of the South American States. Surely there is nothing attractive in such a change, in such a descent.

I conjure you to consider, moreover, that England, without waiting for, and, I am sure, without expecting, so inglorious a retreat on our part, is completing a vast web of ocean steam navigation, based on postage and commerce, that will connect all the European ports, all our own ports, all the South American ports, all the ports in the West Indies, all the ports of Asia and Oceanica, with her great commercial capital. Thus the world is to become a great commercial system, ramified by a thousand nerves projecting from the one head at London. Yet, stupendous as the scheme is, our own merchants, conscious of equal capacity and equal resources, and relying on experience for success, stand here beseeching us to allow them to counteract its fulfilment, and ask of us facilities and aid equal to those yielded by the British Government to its citizens. While our commercial history is full of presages of a successful competition, Great Britain is sunk deep in debt. We are free from debt. Great Britain is oppressed with armies and costly aristocratic institutions ; industry among us is unfettered and free. But it is a contest depending not on armies, nor even on wealth, but chiefly on invention and industry. And how stands the national account in those respects? The cotton-gin, the planing machine, steam navigation, and electrical communication—these are old achievements. England only a year ago invited the nations to bring their inventions and compare them together in a palace of iron and glass. In all the devices for the increase of luxury and indulgence, America was surpassed, not only by refined England and by chivalrous France, but even by semi-barbarian Russia. Not until after all the mortification which such a result necessarily produced, did the comparison of utilitarian inventions begin. Then our countrymen exhibited Dick's Anti-friction Press—a machine that moved a power greater by 240 tons than could be raised by the Brama Hydraulic Press, which, having been used by Sir John Stevenson in erecting the tubular bridge over the Straits of Menai, had been brought forward by the British artisans as a contrivance of unrivalled merit for the generation of direct power.

Next was submitted, on our behalf, the two inventions of St. John, the variation compass, which indicates the deflection of its own needle at any place, resulting from local causes ; and the velocimeter, which tells, at any time, the actual speed of the vessel bearing it, and its distance from the port of departure ; inventions adopted at once by the Admiralty of Great Britain. Then, to say nothing of the ingeniously constructed locks exhibited by Hobbs, which defied the skill of the British artisans, while he opened all of theirs at pleasure, there was Bigelow's power-loom, which has brought down ingrain and Brussels carpets within the reach of the British mechanic and farmer. While the American plows took precedence of all others, McCormick's reaper was acknowledged to be a contribution to the agriculture of England, surpassing in value the cost of the Crystal Palace. Nor were we dishonored in the fine arts, for a well-deserved meed was awarded to Hughes for his successful incorporation in marble of the ideal Oliver Twist; and the palm was conferred on Powers for his immortal statue of the Greek Slave. When these successes had turned away the tide of derision from our country, the yacht America entered the Thames. Skilful architects saw that she combined, in before unknown proportions, the elements of grace and motion, and her modest challenge was reluctantly accepted, and even then only for a tenth part of the prize she proposed. The trial was graced by the presence of the Queen and her Court, and watched with an interest created by national pride and ambition, and yet the triumph was complete.

In the very hour of this, of itself conclusive demonstration of American superiority in utilitarian inventions, and in the art "that leads to nautical dominion," a further and irresistible confirmation was given by the arrival of American clippers from India, freighted at advanced rates with shipments, consigned by the agents of the East India Company at Calcutta to their own warehouses in London. Such and so recent are the proofs, that in the capital element of invention we are equal to the contest for the supremacy of the seas. When I consider them, and consider our resources, of which those of Pennsylvania, or of the valley of the Mississippi, or of California, alone exceed the entire native wealth of Great Britain; when I consider, moreover, our yet unelicited manufacturing capacity—our great population, already nearly equal to that of the British islands, and multiplying at a rate unknown in human progress by accessions from both of the old continents; when I consider the advantages of our geographical position midway between them; and when I consider, above all, the expanding and elevating influence of freedom upon the genius of our people, I feel quite assured that their enterprise will be adequate to the glorious conflict, if it be only sustained by constancy and perseverance on the part of their Government. I do not know that we shall prevail in that conflict; but for myself, like the modest hero who was instructed to charge on the artillery at Niagara, I can say that we "will try;" and that when a difficulty occurs no greater than that which meets us now, my motto shall be the words of the dying commander of the Chesapeake—"Don't give up the ship."

THE COLLINS' STEAMERS.

The policy of the American Government has been for many years to throw their foreign trade and commerce open to the legitimate competition of every flag, and under this policy the shipping and commercial interests of the country were for a time prosperous and satisfactory. Our packet ships were completely successful, and finally got possession of the largest portion of the freight and passenger traffic. Under these circumstances England became anxious, and saw no remedy, but by the establishment of a line of mail steamers to regain what by fair competition she had lost, and therefore commenced such a line of steamers, and placed it wholly under the admiralty jurisdiction, as a government undertaking. They found soon by experience that they could not do it satisfactorily to the public, and the expenses were so enormous, that they considered it good policy to discontinue it.

They then proposed to several intelligent merchants to try the experiment under governmental patronage, and finally after some negotiation Mr. Cunard and his associates entered into a contract in July, 1840, to carry the mails, and for which they were paid £60,000 annually, equal, *a* $4\frac{80}{100}$, to $288,000.

They commenced the service with four steamers, 420 horse power each, and of the capacity or gross tonnage or 4,600 tons, or $62\frac{46}{100}$ per ton, and made at the commencement one passage each month. The Government of Britain soon perceived the importance of this line; it at once changed their position with this country; it gave them a revenue on their mail matter, and on that of the American people. It gave them almost the monopoly of the passenger traffic, and the most valuable of all freights, that upon bullion, and the rich and high priced merchandise of Europe. This far-sighted measure of the British cabinet, at one blow, took from the American packets the three most important items of their business, viz., valuable freights, passengers, and mail money, and thus almost ruined them. The number of sailing packet-

GIDEON, Print.

ships in every port has been lessened, and many of them could not now be kept afloat, were it not for the immense immigration from Ireland and the continent of Europe.

The first six years, England actually derived from the Cunard line of mail steamers a clear revenue of $5,286,800, and the proprietors of this line large profits. The whole nearly was obtained at the expense of American sailing packets, and from the American public, with the aid of the public money of England.

At first this line confined itself to one port; now two ports are used: the company have increased and are increasing the capacity and number of their steamers at the expense of the American people, and this is owing entirely, at the commencement, to the policy of England, in granting them aid to ensure the destruction of all *individual competition* of Americans. The American people and Government felt all this, and through the press, and every other channel, called loudly for an American line of steam packets; the press and people promising to support such a line with money and their patronage. Under these assurances, an American line was built and put into service. The result has been, the American proprietors have built the best ocean mail steamers afloat, in point of strength, speed, and comfort, and have wrested back a portion of the mail money, passenger traffic, and the freights of bullion, and valuable merchandise, and have given general public satisfaction.

No private individuals in the Kingdom of Great Britain, at a time when no opposition was in their way, and when all the trade of America and Europe was open to them, dared at the commencement, begin such an enterprise, knowing as they did the large expenditure of ocean steamers, without substantial aid from the British Government, and the further assurance of indemnity against loss.

The American enterprise was undertaken with four steamers of 1000 horse power each, and of the capacity or gross tonnage of 13,702 tons, for a compensation of $385,000 per annum, or 28$\frac{10}{100}$ per ton, making semi-monthly passages for eight months, and monthly for four months in each year, say twenty passages in all. This was accomplished by a few individuals at an outlay of more than 3,000,000 dollars, in the face of a line with many years of experience, and having the public confidence, and supported by adequate aid from the British treasury, and the patronage of British and American merchants and manufacturers. The British merchants and manufacturers have been *true* to the Cunard line ; they send their merchandise by them, they take passage in them, they send their letters by them, and keep back their duplicates and triplicates for their own line, rather than allow them to go by an American steamer. And the British Government through their agents have done every thing to promote the interest of this line, and have actually charged the inland postage on all of the continental letters going by American steamers, and when by British, the inland postage has been remitted or not charged.

This matter is now before the Postmaster General; and this stroke of management has taken thousands of dollars from the American treasury to the loss and injury of our line of steamers.

This country must always be in competition with Great Britain, and if England opens her treasury to sustain mail lines, then must the United States do the same thing to such of their lines of steamers as come in direct competition with them, or abandon the field, after winning the battle, to their rivals.

If the American line from necessity, that is, the want of means, is compelled to be withdrawn, the consequence must be, the building up of an increased and formidable number of British mail steamers at the expense of the American people. Through such lines they will pay the British Government for the carrying of their letters, and surrender to British capitalists, already made rich by American patronage, all the freights on bullion and valuable merchandise, and the whole of the passenger traffic.

Had England allowed her merchants (without governmental aid at the beginning of ocean steam navigation) to compete legitimately with American merchants, no American merchant would ever have presented himself before an American Congress asking aid against competition with British merchants on the high seas.

There is another very important point of view in which to consider this matter.

Suppose the proprietors of this American line of steamers, for want of the necessary governmental aid, be compelled to relinquish their contract, and to withdraw them from service.

It would be a national disgrace, and would cause much mortification to every American at home and abroad, and great joy and exultation on the other side of the water.

No line of equal capacity and fitness could be again put afloat by individual capitalists.

Where could $3,000,000 of private capital be found? And where are the capitalists able and willing to attempt it?

Let the present line sink, and the Cunard line will then have a complete monopoly, that in time could not be resisted or overcome, unless expelled from our coasts by law. They would have possession of the key of all the commerce of this country with Europe. They would control and raise at will the prices of freights, and the rates of passage, and even the rates of postage of mail-matter would be at their disposal.

The rate of freight, when this line commenced, was £7 10 per ton, now, £4 from England to the United States, and from the United States to England, any rate of freight the shipper chooses to pay, from 6d. to 3s. per barrel. But for this low rate of freight our produce, say, flour, pork, beef, bacon, hams, cheese, lard, butter, apples, &c., &c., could not, at the low prices ruling in Europe, be shipped from this country; and some of them being perishable, can only be shipped by steamers of great speed and good ventilation.

These freights by steamers and sailing packets, constantly on an average rule low, but owing to their departures on regular and specified days, rather than go empty, they take any freight offering; and frequently the freight from New York to Liverpool is actually less than the drayage from the warehouse to the vessel of embarkation.

What has killed the navigation from the St. Lawrence to England, and given millions to the great State of New York, in the shape of tolls on her canals, and employment to her boatmen and laborers, but the low freights and the certainty and expedition of the sailing, and steam packets from New York to Liverpool?

It has transferred a large portion of the products of Canada to the city of New York for a market, and for shipment to Europe, and has actually brought the statesmen of Canada to the very halls of Congress, asking to be placed, as regards exports and imports of the products of both countries, upon a footing of equality.

The cash cost of the Collins' line of steamers, ready for sea, was - - - - -		$2,944,142 71
The following items show the present position of the Collins' line of steamers, viz:		
The amount of stock subscribed is - - -		1,132,000 00
Of which has been paid -	$1,099,900 00	
The Government loan was - -	385,000 00	

The company have borrowed and issued their bonds for - -	700,000 00	
Their floating debt is now, exclusive of interest, about - - -	1,000,000 00	
		3,184,900 00
They have sunk over - - - -		350,000 00

No dividends have been made to the stockholders.

The actual average cost of each voyage to England and back is - -	$65,215 64	
The average receipts of each voyage have been - - - -	48,286 85	
Deficiency each voyage - - - -		16,928 79
Or for 20 voyages - - - - -		$338,574 40

	d.	h.	m.
The shortest passage eastward - - -	9	19	45
The shortest passage westward - - -	9	13	45

Such is the absence of remunerative employment for these steamers in the winter season, that the last steamer, the Atlantic, to England had no freight, and only eight first and nineteen second class passengers.

The estimated expense of keeping four war steamers of the capacity of the Collins' line in commission, exclusive of fuel, is not less than $2,000,000 per annum; and for keeping them in the navy yards ready for sea, $640,000 per annum.

The amount of postage derived exclusively from the Collins' line of steamers from 1st of January to 1st of May, 1851, say 4 months, was $126,606 00, less by $1,727$\frac{38}{100}$ than paid to said line by contract.

The mail service since May has fallen off, owing to the British Government having suddenly increased the mail service of the Cunard line, and consequently *increased* their *pay* considerably.

This move has cut us off from alternating with their line since *May* last, up to which time we shared with them nearly equally all the receipts on mail matter. We must compel them by some new postal arrangement to again alternate with our line, which will give annually to our Post Office over $400,000 to begin with; and this will go on, gradually increasing, until it reaches a million of dollars per annum, and thus create a revenue beyond all the compensation to the steamers,

The policy pursued by the British Government towards their mail steamers has not only secured the numerous collateral public advantages attendant upon their service, but a permanent revenue exceeding the annual outlay. They have found a liberal expenditure the best economy.

Since the foregoing was printed, the following official document has been transmitted from the Postmaster General to the Committee on Naval Affairs of the United States Senate, showing a revenue has been derived, in consequence of the establishment of this line of steamers, up to 31st March last, of $828,675 59 against the contract; which will amount, on the 27th April, 1852, to $770,000—leaving, therefore, a nett gain to the Treasury of $58,675 59.

Exhibit of postage on mails received and sent by the Cunard and Collins' steamers, from Feb. 21st, 1849, to March 31st, 1852.

Postage by Cunard line, from Feb. 21, 1849, to April 27, 1850 - - - - -		$665,311 55
United States portion - -	$138,606 55	
British portion - - -	526,705 00	
	$665,311 55	
Postage by Cunard line, from April 27, 1850, to March 31, 1852 - - - - - -		1,071,302 34
United States portion - -	$223,188 00	
British portion - - -	848,114 34	
	$1,071,302 34	
Postage by Collins' line, from April 27, 1850, to March 31, 1852 - - - - - -		373,337 80
United States portion - -	$326,670 58	
British portion - - -	46,667 22	
	$373,337 80	
		$2,109,951 69

United States revenue for the same period—

1st. By Cunard line, letters, to April 27, 1850 -	$138,606 55
2d. By " " April 27, 1850, to March 31, 1852 - - - - -	223,188 00
3d By Collins' line, letters, April 27, 1850, to March 31, 1852 - - - - -	326,670 58
4th. Newspaper postage, to December 31, 1851 -	46,858 88
5th. Balance on closed mails - - -	90,151 58
6th. Postage for State Department - -	3,200 00
	$828,675 59

The increase of trans-atlantic postage in 1851, over that of 1850, was - - - - -	$197,435 61

Increase by Collins' line -	$183,734 05
Increase by other line -	13,701 56
	$197,435 61

NOTE.—In the preceding statement, the closing mails are estimated for the quarter ending 31st December, 1851, and the newspaper closed mail accounts for the quarter ending 31st March, 1852, and not included.

(Copy.) P. O. DEPARTMENT,
Foreign Desk, April 7, 1852.

I certify, that the above is the copy of the statement from the Auditor's office referred to in the P. M. General's note of to-day's date to E. K. Collins, esq.

(Signed) HORATIO KING.

AMERICAN STEAM NAVIGATION.

SPEECH

OF

HON. GEORGE E. BADGER,

OF NORTH CAROLINA,

FOR

THE COLLINS STEAMERS.

IN SENATE OF THE UNITED STATES, MAY 6, 1852.

WASHINGTON, D. C.:
BUELL & BLANCHARD, PRINTERS.
1852.

AMERICAN STEAM NAVIGATION

SPEECH

OF

HON. GEORGE E. BADGER,

OF NORTH CAROLINA,

FOR

THE COLLINS STEAMERS.

IN SENATE OF THE UNITED STATES, MAY 6, 1852.

WASHINGTON, D. C.:
BUELL & BLANCHARD, PRINTERS.
1852.

SPEECH.

The Senate resumed, as in Committee of the Whole, the consideration of the bill from the House of Representatives, entitled "An act to supply deficiencies in the appropriations for the service of the fiscal year ending the 30th of June, 1852," the pending question being upon the amendment of the Committee on Finance to insert the following:

For additional compensation for increasing the transportation of the United States mail between New York and Liverpool, in the Collins line of steamers, to twenty-six trips per annum, at such times as shall be directed by the Postmaster General, and in conformity to his last annual report to Congress, and his letter of the 15th of November last to the Secretary of the Navy, commencing said increased service on the 1st of January, 1852, at the rate of $33,000 per trip, in lieu of the present allowance, the sum of $236,500.

Mr. BADGER. Mr. President, I desire to submit some observations upon the subject of the amendment before the Senate, and, if no other gentleman is disposed to say anything, I will submit my remarks now. My friend from Virginia, [Mr. HUNTER,] the other day, took occasion to remark that he stood almost alone on this question—most, if not all, of those who had mingled in the debate having taken part in support of the pending amendment. But my friend from Virginia should have remembered that if in number he is but one, in force he is a host. He stands amongst us like Achilles upon the plains of Troy, driving whole battalions before him, and requiring the concentrated energies of a mighty army to arrest his advance. Therefore, he must not be surprised if, when he opposes, many of us should think it necessary that we should support—well knowing that such is the weight and force of his reasoning, the influence of his position, the keen and skilful dexterity of his logic, by which he is able always to "make the worse appear the better reason," it is absolutely necessary that we should summon up all our powers to secure that success to this amendment which we believe its intrinsic merits require.

My friend from Virginia yesterday was pleased to say, in reference to a remark made by the honorable Senator from New York, [Mr. SEWARD,] as to the narrowing influence produced upon the mind by occupying the position of Chairman of the Finance Committee, that, if the suggestion of the Senator from New York were correct, it would be perhaps a happy thing to place me at the head of that committee, as such a narrowing influence might not be amiss upon what he supposed to be the too profuse liberality of my disposition.

Mr. President, there are several difficulties in the way of my occupying the distinguished position to which the partiality of my friend would assign me. In the first place, I do not belong to the right side of this House to assume the direction of any committee. I am much better placed in the capacity of trailing a pike under the command and direction of the honorable Senator from California, [Mr. GWIN,] to whose committee I have been assigned. An experiment was once made by the distinguished gentleman who is now the presiding officer of this body, of placing me at the head of one committee of this body, and an important committee it was. He made me the Chairman of the Committee on Enrolled Bills. But whether it was that I discharged my duties in that high and important position so badly, or neglected them so much, or, as my honorable friend from Michigan says, discharged them so well, and was so critical and careful about the phraseology of our laws—whatever might have been the reason, I seem to have lost caste and credit; for, at the next session, I was summarily displaced from the position of chief in command, and put where I was but a private soldier.

I am by no means ambitious of assuming the position to which my friend from Virginia would assign me; but he will permit me to say, that, if placing me at the head of that committee would have the narrowing influence which he supposes, by equal force of reasoning it seems to me he ought to leave the station which he has assumed; for I know of no gentleman in this body, or in this country, with his high understanding and enlarged views, who needs liberalizing more than he does in regard to the public expenditures of the country for great and noble objects.

Mr. President, the question submitted for the consideration of the Senate is, we all admit, a question of high and controlling importance. It has been said in the course of this discussion that the contest between these two lines has now become a national contest between this country and Great Britain. I desire to amend that statement. From the very moment of the institution of the Collins line, it was a national contest. It has not recently assumed that character. It has always borne it. The enterprise was very far, indeed, from being in fact, or from being regarded by the country, as a mere contest between two rival companies of ship-owners. It was one great, active contest in that mighty drama for the mastery of the seas—for superiority in everything that belongs to strength, speed, effective power, and success for war and for commercial purposes, which long has been, and ever must be, the mightiest contest between this country and Great Britain. After having entered upon this peaceful, and, at the same time, most important contest, the question presented to the American Congress now is, whether we shall dishonorably retrace our steps; whether, when the hand is just stretched out to seize the crown of victory—we shall voluntarily forego all our advantages, retire from the high and eminent position we now occupy in the eyes of all the civilized world, and voluntarily surrender that which to obtain and perpetuate Great Britain would without any hesitation sacrifice a hundred times the amount of money which is involved in the question now before the Senate.

We are now reduced to this position: We must do one of three things; we must either afford the aid which is now asked by this company, and which this amendment proposes to give it; or we must enforce upon it the performance of the contract entered into with this Government, to the utter ruin of its members; or we must permit this line to go down, and permit Great Britain to be, by the acknowledgment of the world, first, not only in naval power, but in naval enterprise, and in national sympathy for her own glory; and to allow her to take possession of the sea by our own voluntary retreat, which, in a fair conflict, the experience of three quarters of a century has shown she never could obtain by skill and power of her own.

I have said that we must do one of these three things; and is it not manifest that one of the three must be done? Why, sir, it is proved; it is not a subject of debate; it does not depend upon minute speculations in arithmetic; it cannot even be necessary to resort to the square-root of my friend from Kentucky to resolve it; but it is proved by clear, distinct, incontrovertible, sworn testimony, that the running of the Collins line, at the present rate of compensation, has brought, on twenty-eight trips, an average loss of nearly $17,000 each trip to the company. Now, it requires nothing to be said to show that it is impossible that the line can be kept up and maintained upon the present rate of compensation, with the loss which must necessarily be thrown upon the intelligent, enterprising, wealthy, and patriotic citizens by whom the line has been established. Gentlemen may say—the honorable gentleman from Virginia has said—that there is not a necessity for this increase of compensation. Gentlemen may say, and gentlemen may think, that the line can be run, and will be run, at the present rate of compensation; but if gentlemen so say and so think, they are greatly deceived. The members of this company are now bearing heavy drafts upon their private funds to meet daily recurring deficiencies, so large that a quarter of a year of them accruing upon persons of ordinary ability would crush them, and which no company, however able, can long sustain.

References have been made to the rate of compensation or assistance afforded by the British Government to the Cunard line; and it has been attempted to be shown that the rate of compensation so given is less than what is proposed to be given by this amendment to sustain the Collins line. Well, suppose it were so; do we not all know that the expenses of maintaining a line, consisting of steamships, depends not so much upon the number as upon the size of the vessels employed? No doubt my friend from Virginia is right in saying that we could maintain a dozen steamers, and send them across the ocean, not merely for twenty-six trips, but for fifty trips, at far less expense than is incurred by the Collins line, even at the present rate of compensation. What the expenses are is to depend upon the size of the vessels engaged. And what is that size? Why, there are four Collins steamers—there are seven Cunarders. The aggregate tonnage of the four Collins steamers exceeds the aggregate tonnage of the seven Cunarders by more than a thousand tons. It is, therefore, no accurate mode of proceeding, to ascertain what amount of expenditure may be needed, to calculate only according to the number of ships and the number of trips. You must take into connection with that the relative size of the vessels employed. Why, sir, in a few years, the wear and tear of these vessels, and the outlay required for the purpose of keeping them afloat, will amount to an actual absorption of the whole principal invested. Permit me to add, also, that another element is to be taken into the account; and that is, the speed with which the vessels traverse the ocean. The more the speed is increased, the greater is the injury to the ship, the more rapidly are the works worn out, and a larger outlay is required for the purpose of keeping her in a running condition. So that it may be very true, that, if we would reduce our ships to the size of the Cunarders; if we would drop them down to a screw propeller, going at the rate of six miles an hour, we might, perhaps, be able to run the vessels, to walk them, or to let them creep, at less money than is required to maintain these large ships, and keep them in that state of proud superiority as to speed which now distinguishes them.

Gentlemen may speculate upon the question, whether these ships ought to cost so much money in maintaining and running them; but the fact is, they do cost it. The fact is, that the expenses exceed the receipts of the company at the rate of nearly $17,000 a trip. Then, what is proposed by this amendment? It is to add, not the $17,000, but we propose to increase the rate of compensation from $19,250 a trip or voyage, to $33,000; that is, we add $13,750 to the compensation allowed for each trip. We hope for better and brighter times. We hope that with this addition these enterprising and patriotic men may be enabled to make good the contest and maintain their superiority. If there be any truth in evidence, if any reliance can be placed upon testimony, the fact is shown that they are losing within a fraction of $17,000 upon every trip. If, therefore, we are to support or assist them at all, it is difficult to conceive what else we could do than to add between $13,000 and $14,000 to the present amount of compensation.

But again, under the additional arrangement entered into by the Post Office and the Navy Departments with these gentlemen, six additional trips have to be made, in order to maintain a constant and equal competition through the winter as well as in the spring and summer months. Then we must recollect, that with regard to these winter trips, besides all the enhanced difficulties which accompany them, they fall greatly short in the ordinary remuneration. The winter freights are small, and the winter passengers are few. So that, putting all these considerations together, I think it must be evident to every gentleman, that if any assistance is to be afforded, that proposed in the amendment is by no means unreasonably large.

Gentlemen may suppose that if this assistance is withheld, this enterprise will still be prosecuted. Permit me to assure them that they are entirely mistaken. So sure as the proposed amendment is rejected, and Congress declines to give the asked for, the desired aid, the very next step will be an application from these gentlemen to be relieved from the ruinous contract into which they have entered with the Government. If we refuse this aid, the other application we cannot deny. It would be unjust and cruelly ungenerous to deny it. No question can remain, but that the moment that application is made to Congress, it will be favorably considered, and promptly granted. Then, how should we stand? The line is to be discontinued! Who would benefit by its discontinuance? English capital, English enterprise, English reputation, and the national honor and glory of England. By whom is the loss to be borne? In each and every one of these particulars it is to be borne by us.

My honorable friend from Virginia said, that if at a single stroke all these Collins steamers were sunk into the bottom of the ocean, there was no doubt but that the Cunard steamers would still bring us the mails. No doubt of that, sir. And does any man doubt, that if the whole American marine were to-morrow gulphed in the depths of the ocean, but that British commercial vessels would still bring us the products of foreign countries, and take away the products of our own? But is there any man here, is there any man in America, whose soul is so dead to the perceptions of national honor and national interest, who would be willing to accept the last alternative? Not my friend from Virginia, I am sure. But, if there be any correctness in the reasoning which he applied to the case of the steamers, the reasoning applies with precisely the same force, and is entitled to just the same weight, in the case to which I apply it. Would anybody be benefited? Why, surely not, sir. Would the vessels engaged in prosecuting, under sail and without the aid of steam, the commercial pursuits of the United States gain the advantage of discontinuing this line? Surely they would not, sir. The passengers would then go by the Cunard line from this country to England, and from England here. And why? Because, in the rage for rapid motion now prevailing, men will always travel by that conveyance which gives them the speediest transmission from one end of their journey to the other. Would sailing vessels be benefited with regard to freights by the discontinuance of this line? Surely not; for the freights which are transmitted by the Collins line would then, for a very obvious reason, be transmitted by the Cunard line. If the Collins line were put out of the way, there would be no effectual competition in regard to freights between ordinary sail-vessels and steam-vessels. The steamers carry those freights which are of comparative lightness and of increased value. The ordinary heavy freights, which seek sure and cheap transmission, cannot afford to bear the additional expense of steamer transportation.

My friend from Virginia mentioned yesterday that he understood from some persons concerned in iron works, that these steamers had actually brought over iron at so small a rate as almost to put it on the footing of taking it in for ballast. Now, I think my friend's informant must have been mistaken. I learn from a source which is, I think, entitled to the highest credit, that not one ton of iron has ever been brought in these steamers as ballast. They do not want ballast, with the immense weight of their machinery, with the immense quantities of coal which they carry. One great object is to reduce the amount of pressure, and to enable them to move, therefore, with more rapidity. Sail vessels are in the habit often of carrying articles in that way, because when they are solid and heavy, it relieves them from the necessity of cumbering themselves with the ballast which they would otherwise require.

Then it seems to me that the discontinuance of this line involves the certain consequence of giving the whole steam communication between this country and Great Britain, and, as a consequence of it, the steam communication between this country and the continent of Europe, into the hands of British steamship owners. There is no escape from it.

If I were now to suppose that a large outlay would be required during the whole continuance of this contract, for a very small remuneration in the form of postages to the United States, I should, for one, be exceedingly unwilling to see this line go down. I do not exactly agree with my friend from Virginia. I do not believe that money is devoted to its proper purposes by being hoarded. I do not believe that money expended to advance the honor, to promote the interests, to maintain the supremacy of my own country, is ever otherwise than well and effectually bestowed—bringing that return which nations should consider as the highest and the best, the improvement of the condition of their people, the elevation of the character of the whole; for with regard to nations the reputation of strength is strength. He who has established a character of invincibility will not be very likely to have his pretensions put to the test by an actual conflict. Nothing, undoubtedly, supports individual States more in the world than the reputation of perseverance, strength, and inflexible integrity. But, then, is there any reason to suppose that we shall be left in such a situation?

My friend from Virginia does not believe that this line will be so prosecuted, or can be so prosecuted, as to make an adequate return to the Treasury, in the shape of postages, for the expenditures which will be involved. Now, upon what is that founded? In all our domestic concerns, have we not ever found that the postages of the country are upon the increase, that every facility given to correspondence increases correspondence, and that just and reasonable reductions upon the prices of postage are followed by a large increase in the amount received from postages? Postal arrangements by steam-vessels are now in their beginning. They are just in the commencement, where they are showing us what they will do. I entertain a strong and confident expectation and hope, that if we give the required assistance to this line, it will be able to maintain itself, and overmaster the competition in which it is now engaged; and that in a few years we shall have not only the satisfaction of knowing that our country has maintained, increased, and consolidated its reputation in the eyes of the world as a great naval power, as a nation of enterprise and untiring perseverance, and that even in a pecuniary point of view we shall receive the just reward of this high and elevated course of conduct, by having immense amounts of money poured into the Treasury. What has been the increase already? Why, the increase of the line to Havre the year before, makes nearly $200,000. Who shall set bounds to it? No one.

If, therefore, it were to be viewed solely as a question of dollars and cents—as the outlay of money with the expectation of a return in money—I think the case is one which, if my friend from Virginia would bring his peculiar tact to bear of calculating, which, as the Chairman of the Committee on Finance, he ought to do, how much will be received for a given sum laid out, he will see that even upon that mode of treating this subject, and keeping a careful and watchful eye upon the Treasury, we are likely to bring a great deal more into it than will be paid out of it by this proposition.

Then, Mr. President, there are other considerations connected with this matter. These are war steamers. They enable us not only to accomplish the mastery and to insure victory in the peaceful contest of skill and enterprise in which we are now embarked, but they are well calculated, in the event of another and bloody contest, to enable us to maintain in that the same superiority. My friend from Virginia thinks that they are not calculated for war steamers. I have heretofore said, on another occasion, that I should consider them as capable of being efficient vessels of war until the contrary had been demonstrated by experiment. And why, sir? They were built for vessels of war—they were built under the direction of the Navy Department, directed and superintended by all the skill in naval construction of which that Department is master. Every requisition made by Government in their construction was fully and completely complied with; and with regard to strength, the requirements of the Department were even exceeded by the proprietors of the line.

Mr. HUNTER. I dislike to interrupt the gentleman, but does he mean to say that these steamers are built of white oak, as ships of war are built?

Mr. BADGER. I said they were built according to the requisitions of the Navy Department. Although I once had the honor to be at the head of the Navy Department, I do not claim for myself a perfect acquaintance with all the details of naval armament. I do not say that I have not the time, but I have not the energy of my friend from Virginia, to make myself acquainted with these particulars. I take my position here. I have no skill in such matters; I pretend to none. These vessels were built under the direction of an act of Congress, which required that they should be built under the superintendence of the Navy Department. They were built under the supervision of the proper officers of the Navy Department—those officers to whom the Government trusts when it builds ships of its own, to see that they have the necessary qualities. I suppose that, when my friend used the term "white oak," he did not mean "white oak," but "live oak." I understand from my friend from Rhode Island, [Mr. CLARKE,] who comes from a quarter of country where every man understands these matters, even Senators, that they are built of white oak, though not of live oak.

Mr. HUNTER. The Senator from Florida, [Mr. MALLORY,] who is acquainted with these subjects, tells me that they are planked with pine, and not with white oak, as is usual with vessels of war.

Mr. BADGER. Well, sir, I was not speaking of planking. I was speaking of timbers.

Mr. HUNTER. The strength of vessels depends in some degree on the planking.

Mr. BADGER. I wish my friend from Florida would get up and give his testimony now.

Mr. MALLORY. What testimony is it?

Mr. BADGER. I do not know. You are not my witness. [Laughter.]

Mr. MALLORY. If the question is what the steamers are planked with, I will say that every ship that I have happened to know anything about, built under naval directions, has been planked with oak planks. The Collins steamers are planked with pine. If they are not, they have been officially misrepresented. The timbers and frames of naval vessels are live oak, and the timbers and frames of the Collins steamers are a mixture of live oak, locust, and pine.

Mr. BADGER. Well, be it so. I would ask the Senator from Florida one question. He says these steamers are planked with pine. Are they not planked with Southern pine?

Mr. MALLORY. Certainly, sir.

Mr. BADGER. Enough said. If they are planked with Southern *pine*, it is a great *deal* better than Northern oak. [Laughter.]

Mr. MALLORY. All I have to say is, that it has not been so considered by the naval authorities of this country, who have uniformly preferred oak.

Mr. BADGER. That is because they have inclined to Northern interests. I am very happy to say that they are coming round. I am for Southern pine against Northern oak. The naval constructors had the direction of these vessels, they were approved by them, and they were accepted by the Department. As I have said, and now repeat, I shall consider them as competent steam war-vessels, until, by some experiments, the contrary shall be shown. Nothing can be urged against this but opinion. My friend from New Jersey [Mr. MILLER] the other day read two brief opinions upon this subject—one from the naval constructor, and the other from one of the most eminent gentlemen who belong to the Navy.

Commodore Perry, in a letter to the Secretary of the Navy, says:

"According to my calculations, the cost of the conversion of either the beforementioned vessels, exclusive of armaments, repair of machinery, &c., would not, or certainly ought not, to cost for each steamer over $20,000; and it could readily be done for this at any of our navy yards. With respect to the description and weight of their respective armaments, I am clearly of the opinion that the first-class steamers already named could easily carry four 10-inch Paixhan guns on pivots—two forward and two aft—of the weight of those in the Mississippi, and ten 8-inch Paixhan guns on the sides; and this armament would not incommode the vessels, and the weight less than the ice, which is usually forty tons, and stowed away in one mass."

Again, he says:

"In the general operations of a maritime war they could render good service, and especially would they be useful from their great speed as dispatch vessels, and for the transportation of troops, always capable of attack and defence and of overhauling or escaping from an enemy.

"The Atlantic, Pacific, Baltic, and Arctic, have all been built, inspected, and received by the Navy Department."

My friend from New Jersey also read a letter of Mr. Grice, very well known for his skill as a naval constructor. He says, in a letter to the Chairman of the Committee on Naval Affairs:

UNITED STATES NAVY YARD, PHILADELPHIA, *April* 14, 1852.

SIR: In answer to yours of the 13th, I have to state, as chief naval constructor, the specifications for building the Collins line of steamers were submitted to me, and approved, as in accordance with the act of 3d March, 1847.

They can be converted into war-steamers to carry a battery equal to our largest steam frigates, in a short time, and the necessary alterations to be made to receive such a battery will not exceed a cost of $20,000 each.

I am, sir, with great respect, your obedient servant,

FRANCIS GRICE.

To the Hon. WILLIAM M. GWIN, *United States Senate, Washington.*

We have, then, the opinion of Commodore Perry, that these vessels, in case of a general maritime war, would be exceedingly valuable, not merely as transports, as my friend from Virginia seemed to suppose, but that they would be pre-eminently valuable for war purposes, from two considerations—first, their superiority of speed; and, secondly, their power both of attack and defence.

But my friend from Virginia seemed to be of opinion that speed was not any recommendation to a war vessel. "What," said he, "do we prepare our ships with speed in order that they may run away from an enemy?" I answer, Yes, when there is occasion to run; and we should furnish them with speed to overtake an enemy when there is occasion to overtake him. However dignified and lofty it may sound for a gentleman to say that he does not think it a recommendation that one of our ships of war should have speed to escape from an enemy, yet tried by its practical application to things, every man knows that there are occasions in the history of all bodies of men, whether they serve by land or by sea, where nothing is of more importance than to have speed, in order to escape a foe whom they cannot overmaster or successfully resist. My friend from Virginia should recollect that the very speed which enables them to escape a superiority of force, carries them also with triumphant power and unexpected suddenness, which gives additional force to the attack upon an enemy whom it is desirable to meet, and against whom they are capable of successfully contending.

It seems to me, then, that in either view of the subject, first considering these vessels as mere instrumentalities for the transmission of intelligence, and maintaining our postal arrangements, we have every reason to believe that the money which this amendment proposes to give, in addition to their present compensation, will be amply remunerated to us; and, in the second place, if this were not so, we have, what is of great importance to us, the four largest and fleetest steamers in the world, ready at any and all times to be incorporated into our warlike marine. The Senator from Virginia talks about there being six or eight weeks required for preparing them for war purposes. Now, they can be speedily prepared, and at a very small cost. What that "speed" means is very readily shown by the extracts which were read yesterday by the Senator from Texas, [Mr. Rusk,] showing that, in the British service, the change of steamers into vessels for war purposes was accomplished in three days, when it was desirable to convert them into vessels of war.

But, in order to avoid any difficulty whatever in regard to the supposed loss which the Government is ultimately to sustain, I have an amendment which I mean to propose, if the Senate shall adopt the amendment now under consideration, as a proviso, for transferring to the Post Office Department the charge of this line of steamers, and supposing it should result in such great loss, after a fair experiment has been tried upon the subject, authorizing Congress to discontinue the contract. This, I think, will relieve the amendment of all reasonable objections. I have no fear, myself, that Congress will ever be called upon to exert such a power. On the contrary, I believe that the longer the line exists and is maintained, the more the hearts of the people will cluster around it as a source of national advantage and national pride.

There is, however, Mr. President, one other objection which has been sometimes urged against this amendment. It is said that, supposing the amendment to be proper in itself—supposing it is proper to be adopted upon a suitable bill, and at a suitable time, it is not a proper amendment to put upon this bill. Upon that subject I wish to say a few words. This is a bill to supply deficiencies in the appropriations for the service of the present half fiscal year. In my opinion, the amendment is in itself proper, and suitable to this bill. It will be recollected that, during the recess of Congress, the heads of the Post Office and Navy Departments came to an arrangement or understanding with the proprietors of the Collins line, that they should increase the trips from twenty to twenty-six per annum; that they should commence the increased service on the first of January last, and that they should trust to Congress affirming what had been done, and for fixing the rate of additional compensation, if any should be given. The subject was brought to our attention by reports from the proper Departments. Now, if Congress think proper to give their sanction to this arrangement, there is a deficiency in the appropriations made at the last session for this half fiscal year. I cannot conceive why this provision is not as appropriate to this bill as any of the other provisions which are contained in it. True, sir, the necessity for this appropriation did not exist when the general appropriation bill was passed; true, the arrangement which has caused this deficiency has been made since the close of the last session of Congress; true, it has arisen under a conditional understanding and agreement, subject to the ratification of Congress; but still, if we are disposed to ratify it, we give it validity and effect from the commencement, and thereby produce the very deficiency which this appropriation is intended to supply. But suppose that it is not so. Forms must yield to substance. There is a necessity sometimes for disregarding the ordinary routine in which business is discharged, and to accomplish what is necessary at the time and in the manner in which it can alone be accomplished. Now, if this amendment is not put here, it will be too late. The moment it is rejected, we shall be called upon by this company to discharge them from the obligation of running the line which they are now running at such ruinous sacrifices—a call which we cannot, without great injustice and want of generosity, resist. The consequence will be, if this amendment is thrown out upon an idea that it is not appropriate to the bill now pending before the Senate, that the line will go down.

I had in my possession a few days ago (and which, I am very sorry to say, I have lost) a letter addressed to my honorable friend from New York, [Mr. Fish,] by a very distinguished citizen of this country, well known as once a member of the other House from the State of New York—well known for being one of the most liberal, intelligent, and enterprising of American merchants for many years. I mean Moses H. Grinnell. He wrote a letter to my friend from New York upon the subject of this line, and with that letter I had proposed to support, as by authority, some of the suggestions which I have ventured to throw out. I have unfortunately mislaid it. In that letter he says, to my friend, it might be supposed that the maintenance of this line would operate injuriously upon the large packet interests in which he is concerned. But he says that he wishes him distinctly to understand that his pride as an American would never permit him to suffer any such paltry interests of his own to stand in the way of the maintenance of a line which was reflecting such distinguished honor and bringing such distinguished advantage to the country. Besides, he says that even that view must be considered to a great extent fallacious; because, if this line were discontinued, it would do nothing for the sailing packets, but would merely throw what is now transported of passengers and of freight by the Collins line entirely in the hands of the English steamers.

He makes another remark, that enterprising and intelligent merchants who look far ahead—further, I believe, than politicians or even statesmen, for their horizon is generally bounded by the approaching Presidential election, and we are too much in the habit of controlling our views and circumscribing our patriotism by considerations connected with the advance or defeat of a particular party—see, in the present condition of Europe, symptoms of such an outbreak there as may necessarily involve the removal, temporarily at least, of the Cunard steamers from the purposes to which they are now devoted; and, if then the Collins line should go down, one of the greatest benefits to commerce that this country or the world has ever experienced—that of speedy, prompt, almost instantaneous, communication between Europe and this country, would be entirely destroyed. So that, in any event, whatever may be the case, he is clearly of opinion that the honor and the interests of the country equally require that Congress should give it such aid as is necessary to enable it effectually to succeed—not doled out with a grudging hand, but given with the spirit of men who realize what is their duty to themeelves and their country, and who are resolved to discharge it.

Mr. President, I have occupied rather more time than I intended upon this subject. I wish to conclude by merely saying that though personally I am as far removed from any connection with, or any immediate advantage from, the Collins line, and all the various facilities it affords, as any other gentleman on this floor, and perhaps as any other gentleman in this country, yet as an American citizen I should deeply regret to see that line go down. I should regret it, from a just and honest pride in the superiority of my country—regret it, from an eager and anxious desire to see all her interests developed, and to see her growing in wealth, and in power, and in reputation. If we give this assistance, and if, having supported this line with all the available means in our power, we should at last, in a fair contest, be beaten by our English rival, I should regret that, deeply regret it; but I should feel that we had suffered no disgrace; for he who does all he can, and is overmastered, may be unfortunate, but he can never be looked upon with contempt. But if we voluntarily recede from the undertaking in which we are embarked—if we withhold the necessary aid—if we say to England, "Take possession of this great line; we retire from the contest; be you the mistress of the seas in the estimation of all the world, and let us sink into a secondary, contemptible position"—if we should do that, I should feel that we had not only committed a false step, had not only lost what we might have maintained, but had covered ourselves with dishonor. From that I hope my country will ever be safe.

www.ingramcontent.com/pod-product-compliance
Lightning Source LLC
LaVergne TN
LVHW021407110826
845150LV00007B/1818

* 9 7 8 1 4 2 5 5 1 2 3 0 9 *